7

SPIRITUAL
DISCIPLINES
TO HELP YOU
GROW IN
YOUR FAITH

WORSHIP
Scripture
SOLITUDE
fasting

FEED
THE
DOG

MINISTRY
prayer
COMMUNITY

BROCK
GILL

LifeWay Press®
Nashville, Tennessee

LifeWay | Students

ISBN: 978146271042

Item: 005796736

Dewey decimal classification: 248.83

Subject headings: RELIGION / CHRISTIAN MINISTRY / YOUTH

To order additional copies of this resource, write to LifeWay Resources Customer Service; One LifeWay Plaza; Nashville, TN 37234-0113; fax 615.251.5933; phone toll free 800.458.2772; order online at www.lifeway.com; email orderentry@lifeway.com;or visit the LifeWay Christian Store serving you.

Printed in the United States of America.

Student Ministry Publishing

LifeWay Resources

One LifeWay Plaza

Nashville, TN 37234

ABOUT THE AUTHOR

Brock has set the pace for a new generation of edgy, daring illusionists as he amazes audiences with his unique stage show, dry wit, and mind-blowing escapes.

With a passion for reaching people with the gospel truth that changed his own life, Brock went back to college and began performing at church outreach events. News of his creative method of evangelism quickly spread and he began to receive invitations almost immediately.

Since those first events, God has taken Brock's ministry across the United States and the globe, and his heart for the lost has grown. Understanding that people have short attention spans and a desire to be entertained visually, he has learned how to quickly draw in an audience and keep them on the edge of their seats. Brock's message for Christ is clear and effective. He has seen God touch many lives through his ministry.

A major highlight of Brock's career was the release of a documentary called "The Miracles of Jesus." Produced by British Broadcasting Company (BBC) and Discovery Channel, this project gave Brock the opportunity to objectively investigate firsthand the miracles of Jesus in the New Testament. Brock took on the role of lead investigator for the project, an assignment that took him all the way to Israel and Malta. The three-hour program debuted on Discovery Channel.

One thing is for certain—a Brock Gill show will be a memorable experience because of his grand illusions, death-defying stunts, subtle comedy, and unique presentation of the gospel.

SPIRIT AND FLESH

What comes to mind when you hear the word *discipline*? Most people today don't like this word—it conjures up images of punishments like going to time-out or serving a detention. Discipline does not always refer to punishment. It can also refer to the practice of training ourselves in a skill. We all discipline ourselves in various ways. The athlete disciplines herself by running every day and eating high-protein foods. The musician disciplines himself by practicing every day and memorizing notes and chord progressions. The satisfaction of doing anything with excellence only comes to those who put in the work. The same is true of our walks with Christ. If you want to walk in the fullness of joy promised to followers of Jesus, you must learn the value of discipline and commit to faithfully doing the things that lead to spiritual growth and joy in Christ. In *Feed the Dog*, we will unpack seven key practices or disciplines that will help us grow in our relationship with the God who made us. These disciplines will guide us to live out His purpose for our lives.

HOW TO USE

VIDEO GUIDE – Begin each group session by watching the video from Brock Gill that's included in the Leader Kit. Read the Scriptures together and discuss the questions that follow.

GROUP DISCUSSION – Each session unpacks the value and impact of one spiritual discipline. Group leaders will want to read through this section carefully, reviewing each discussion question to prepare to guide students during group time.

DEVOTIONS – There are six one-page personal devotions for group members included in each session. Encourage group members to set aside at least 10-15 minutes each day for completing these devotions. Instruct students to jot down questions they might have so you can address any concerns in the next group time.

LEADER GUIDE – The Leader Guide at the end of this resource contains the main point of each session, an optional activity or illustration to introduce the session, and a challenge to help students engage in the discipline covered in each session on their own.

1

SPIRIT AND FLESH

VIDEO
GUIDE

Start by watching the video for Session 1. It begins with an illusion and Brock introducing the study. He shares about the two natures every believer has and how we are called to feed the spirit.

BROCK SHARES THE SECRET TOOLS JEAN-EUGENE ROBERT-HOUDIN HAD AND HOW HE CHANGED THE COURSE OF HISTORY BECAUSE OF THE TIME HE SPENT PRACTICING. Spiritual disciplines require the investment of work and time. It takes time for us to be more and more like Jesus. We have to set our minds on feeding the spirit rather than the flesh (Col. 3:2).

> *What comes to mind when you hear the word "discipline"?*
>
> *Do you tend to see spiritual disciplines as more of a duty or a delight?*

Think about worship, Scripture, prayer, solitude, fasting, ministry, and community. Are these spiritual disciplines a big part of your life now? What spiritual disciplines do you want to grow in?

> *List some things you want to learn or gain from this study.*
>
> *How will you seek to practice the spiritual disciplines this week?*

IN 1967 MY FATHER WAS IN COLLEGE AND HAD JUST MET A GIRL WHO WOULD EVENTUALLY BECOME MY MOM. At the end of the semester, he went home to see his family in south Louisiana. As he pulled into the driveway, he saw his dad standing at the door with a worried look on his face. My dad knew the reason for his concern before he even got out of his car. His father (my grandfather) was holding a letter. My dad had been drafted by the United States Army and had ten days to report to base.

Dad withdrew from college and quickly found himself in the jungle of Vietnam. He was given a beautiful German Shepherd named Fritz. His first assignment was to feed the dog and then the training began. Every day my dad fed, trained, and played with Fritz. In a short time, that dog became his closest companion. Fritz even saved my dad's life. My dad's job was to walk the perimeter of the Army base by himself at night with nothing more than his M-16 rifle and his trusted dog. He felt alone and was often scared, but he trusted his dog. After all, Fritz could smell and hear the enemy coming long before anyone else.

One night, some soldiers near the perimeter fell asleep in a bunker. They never woke up and the enemy slipped in and killed them in their sleep. My dad knew he could never fall asleep. He and the dog had to stay alert. He made sure he and his dog were always healthy because their lives depended on it.

My father still recalls the last day he spent in Vietnam. He had to say goodbye to his best friend, Fritz, who had saved his life so many times. He fed his dog and then jumped onto a helicopter and went home.

As I listen to my dad's story of his time in the military, I think about how the dog was taken care of and healthy because of how invaluable he was. Fritz would save him from the schemes of the enemy.

Similarly, there was a man who had two dogs. The dog he fed became the biggest and healthiest. Likewise, every follower of Christ has two natures: spirit and flesh. Whichever one we feed will grow to be the biggest.

In everything we do, we are either feeding our spirit or our flesh. Our behaviors and disciplines (or lack of) provide nourishment to either our spirit-side or flesh-side of our soul.

Whatever you take in—food or TV or something else—will show up in your life. For example, I have a friend who loves to watch TV. She will often watch an entire season of a show in one day while lying on her couch. I noticed that when she does, her language and thinking change. Her attitude mimics the TV shows she's watching. I remember when she was having a tough time at her job and she began thinking about what she wanted to do and where she wanted to live. She then explained that she was considering working for the CIA. I thought it was a bit strange because she had no background in that type of work. It turns out she was watching popular TV shows with female actors in the CIA! The show she filled her days with caused her to want to make major changes in her life.

If you consistently fill your mind with something, you think about that thing all the time. I am not saying we should never watch TV, but we certainly should think carefully about the things we give our attention to and fill our minds with. Do they feed the flesh, or do they feed the Spirit?

WHAT IS THE FLESH?

"Flesh" is commonly used by Paul, the author of the Book of Romans, to refer to sinful nature. Flesh is the worldly side of us that is bent toward sin. The flesh is the opposite of the Spirit and is against God. Flesh is self-centered and looks to please man rather than God. Simply put, flesh is the sinful nature. When we think life is all about doing what we want and living for ourselves, we are living in the flesh. Our flesh is the rebellious nature. As F. F. Bruce said, "The flesh . . . is doomed to die."[1]

WHAT IS THE SPIRIT?

When we choose to follow Christ, He dwells inside of us through the Holy Spirit. He puts His Spirit in us. That Spirit is life. The Spirit is the One who leads us to desire God, obey God, and to love Him. The Spirit prays for us—He is on our side.

As Christ-followers, the Spirit of God is alive inside of us. When the Spirit is in us, we will produce the fruit of the Spirit (Gal. 5:22-23). When we sin, we are living in the flesh. We must train ourselves to walk in the Spirit with a prayerful mind and a heart that is submissive to God.

By feeding the Spirit, we are not literally giving food to the Holy Spirit. Rather, we are submitting to the working of the Spirit. When we "feed" the Spirit, then we starve the flesh. Feeding the Spirit or the flesh means we give it attention. We must, as Paul says, not "make plans to gratify the desires of the flesh" (Rom. 13:14).

READ ROMANS 8:13.

> *. . . because if you live according to the flesh (sinful nature), you are going to die. But if by the Spirit you put to death the deeds of the body (flesh), you will live.*

Compare the fruit of the flesh (Gal. 5:16-18,19-20) to the fruit of the Spirit (Gal. 5:22-23). What happens when we give attention to each?

Our spirit and flesh are willing to eat as much as we feed them. It's up to us to be disciplined enough to know how and what to feed. Whatever we spend time thinking about, watching, listening to, talking about, and so on, reveals the condition of our hearts. If someone reads car magazines every day, then he or she will likely long for a nicer car. If someone is reading and understanding Scripture daily, then it is more likely that he or she will be thinking about spiritual things and have the wisdom provided by God's Word.

Read the following passage from Galatians 5:16-18.

I say then, walk by the Spirit and you will certainly not carry out the desire of the flesh. For the flesh desires what is against the Spirit, and the Spirit desires what is against the flesh; these are opposed to each other, so that you don't do what you want. But if you are led by the Spirit, you are not under the law.

Why is it so important for us to walk by the Spirit? How do we do this?

The flesh is always hungry. It's willing to eat whatever trash you feed it. Sometimes it's not so obvious that our food is not good for us. Sometimes we feed our flesh things that seem okay, or good enough, or not harmful. Remember that good is not best. God has what's best, but often we settle for good enough. We must starve the flesh, rather than feed it.

Read the following verses: Romans 8:7-8, 13:14; Galatians 5:19-22. What does each passage say about the flesh and the consequences that follow when we feed it?

The flesh is hostile to God. It's simple: If you live by the flesh, then you are not and will not be pleasing God. This should bother you. It should get your attention.

The flesh desires sin. It's obvious. These verses make clear that there is fruit of the flesh and fruit of the Spirit. Look at the list, and determine which type of life you want to have today, two years from now, or even ten years from now. I personally want a life that is pleasing to God and one that produces the fruit of the Spirit.

So, what action steps can we take to make sure we feed the Spirit instead of the flesh? Here's where the spiritual disciplines come into play.

WHAT ARE SPIRITUAL DISCIPLINES?

The spiritual disciplines are essential to your faith in Christ—these practices help you grow in your walk with the Lord. Think of these as adventures or as the growth process on your journey with Jesus rather than as chores. Think of the spiritual disciplines as nourishment for your soul and enjoy the time and process of implementing these practices in your daily life.

Have you ever wondered why some people seem to grow in the faith and others fall away? Have you noticed people in your church or school who have made commitments to follow Christ but later seem to be just as worldly as the next?

How can you make sure your walk with Christ is genuine?

I believe the difference between those who live for God after high school (or today) and those who do not, can be traced back to these disciplines. If you avoid these things, in a few short years you can expect to not be living a life of faith. However, if you practice these things, you will grow to become the man or woman God has called you to be. The disciplines are not fruit, values, ideas, or intentions. The disciplines are things you do—you have to act!

So, what are these specific disciplines? I could list many, but let's focus on seven. These seven practices are essential to growing in your faith:

- worship
- Scripture
- prayer
- solitude

- fasting
- ministry
- community

Get ready. Through truth and practicing these spiritual disciplines, you will be equipped to feed the right dog—the spirit, not the flesh.

"Two natures beat within my breast
The one is foul, the one is blessed
The one I love, the one I hate
The one I feed will dominate." [2]
–Anonymous

ALTHOUGH BY THIS TIME YOU OUGHT TO BE TEACHERS, YOU NEED SOMEONE TO TEACH YOU THE BASIC PRINCIPLES OF GOD'S REVELATION AGAIN. YOU NEED MILK, NOT SOLID FOOD. NOW EVERYONE WHO LIVES ON MILK IS INEXPERIENCED WITH THE MESSAGE ABOUT RIGHTEOUSNESS, BECAUSE HE IS AN INFANT. BUT SOLID FOOD IS FOR THE MATURE—FOR THOSE WHOSE SENSES HAVE BEEN TRAINED TO DISTINGUISH BETWEEN GOOD AND EVIL.

HEBREWS 5:12-14

I love motorcycles. For a few years, I was an amateur motocross racer and it was the most fun I've ever had. But, not all of it was enjoyable. It was hard work and there were trials along the way.

One weekend I was racing in an endurance race in Kentucky. It was a hot September day, and we were to race through the woods for over two hours, nonstop. Motocross racing is among the most physically demanding sports on the planet. Every muscle is used and your heart rate increases rapidly.

I thought I was prepared. I had just trained for and run a half marathon and was in good shape. I had plenty of water and sports drinks. But, as the race progressed, I became extremely tired. Many other competitors had dropped out due to exhaustion, but I continued.

Near the end, I heard other motorcycles behind me revving their engines as a signal for me to slow down to let them pass me, but no one was there. I was hallucinating. It was weird. I continued until I crossed the finish line, but I got off my bike and could not talk. It turned out that I was close to having a heat stroke because I pushed my body too hard and didn't drink enough fluids.

The lesson for me here was simple: I needed to drink more fluids and eat the right foods to keep my body healthy. The same goes for our spiritual lives. What we consume will either make us healthy or sick. We need to feed ourselves good, nutritious, spiritual food in order for us to grow in godliness.

Have you ever been thirsty or dehydrated physically? What about spiritually?

What is the good, spiritual food and drink that you need to make a part of your daily life? Are you already practicing some of the spiritual disciplines? If not, how will you make them a part of your life this week?

I SAY THEN, WALK BY THE SPIRIT AND YOU WILL CERTAINLY NOT CARRY OUT THE DESIRE OF THE FLESH. FOR THE FLESH DESIRES WHAT IS AGAINST THE SPIRIT, AND THE SPIRIT DESIRES WHAT IS AGAINST THE FLESH; THESE ARE OPPOSED TO EACH OTHER, SO THAT YOU DON'T DO WHAT YOU WANT.

GALATIANS 5:16-17

How do we walk by the Spirit as Galatians 5:16 instructs us to do? Which side, the Spirit or the flesh, are you feeding the most? How can you tell?

A man had two dogs; the one he fed grew the biggest.

We have spirit and flesh. We need to feed the right dog. Let me explain. I am not literally saying that the Holy Spirit is a dog. Think of it as you would if you had two dogs. What would happen if you fed one and not the other? One would starve and eventually die. Now, apply this metaphor to your spiritual life.

What areas or parts of your life are of the flesh and need to be starved?

My wife and I are away from home over 200 days of the year, so we don't have any pets or plants, or anything else that requires feeding or tending to. One time we decided to get one of those bamboo plants because we were told that they require almost no attention. So, my wife promised to water it and keep it alive. Guess what? It died. So we bought another one and another and another. They all died. Why? Because we were not around to tend to them. We didn't keep them watered. We killed multiple plants that were supposed to be impossible to kill.

Neglect or time away will kill just about anything. We can't neglect our spirit. Feeding the right dog takes discipline. This doesn't come naturally, so we must be intentional. If we neglect feeding the spirit, then the flesh will naturally grow. And you know what? It will grow out of control. In the coming weeks, you will learn how to feed your spirit so that you will grow to have a strong and healthy spiritual life.

Have you ever forgotten to feed or water a plant or a pet? What happened?

Why is it so important for us to make the spiritual disciplines a regular habit in our lives? List some action steps you will take to remind yourself to feed the spirit instead of the flesh.

LET US WALK WITH DECENCY, AS IN THE DAYTIME: NOT IN CAROUSING AND DRUNKENNESS; NOT IN SEXUAL IMPURITY AND PROMISCUITY; NOT IN QUARRELING AND JEALOUSY. BUT PUT ON THE LORD JESUS CHRIST, AND DON'T MAKE PLANS TO GRATIFY THE DESIRES OF THE FLESH.

ROMANS 13:13-14

Three things I like are pizza, chocolate, and ice cream. But I really like pie.

Generally I try to eat foods that are healthy though, and most of the time I stick to this philosophy. There are times, however, like vacation, celebrations, or Thanksgiving where I go crazy and eat all of the things I like without counting calories or thinking about the consequences. Over the years I've seen a pattern. Typically I will only eat poorly for a few days around Thanksgiving but after a few days my will is weak. My appetite for unhealthy food begins to take over. I generally continue eating things that are filled with sugar a few days after Thanksgiving. That turns into Christmas and soon I realize that my eating habits have completely changed and I am saying *yes* to all kinds of foods I used to say *no* to.

How does this happen? Lack of discipline is the short answer. Every January I find myself with extra pounds and tight-fitting pants and it's not until I literally feel the effect of my eating habits that I am motivated to change.

Your flesh, your sin nature, is kind of like my appetite around Thanksgiving. It will always be hungry. No matter how much you feed your flesh, it will never be satisfied. It always wants more than you can feed it and the results are never good. Your flesh does not have your good in mind (1 Pet. 2:11).

READ ROMANS 13:13-14 AGAIN.

In these verses, I see a clear picture of the flesh. And in the last part of verse 14, Paul tells us to not even consider how to gratify the desires of the flesh, but rather to clothe ourselves with Jesus!

> *How are you most tempted to feed your flesh? How will you clothe yourself with Jesus this week?*

> *List some ways you will practice the spiritual disciplines and make them a daily part of your life.*

BUT THE FRUIT OF THE SPIRIT IS LOVE, JOY, PEACE, PATIENCE,
KINDNESS, GOODNESS, FAITHFULNESS, GENTLENESS, AND SELF-
CONTROL. THE LAW IS NOT AGAINST SUCH THINGS.

GALATIANS 5:22-23

Recently I traveled to Central America for some of my shows. We journeyed way out onto an island off the coast of Nicaragua known as Rama. We arrived at a small community where we would do a show and share the gospel with the local people there.

My team and I grew extremely tired and thirsty from our extended travel and lack of sleep. We started getting grumpy (maybe a little *hangry* too). At that point we realized we were dehydrated and water was not enough to keep up with the demands of the hot and humid climate.

A local man said "follow me." He took us across the island into an area filled with coconut, mango, and other fruit trees. The people began to climb up and cut off pieces of fruit for us to eat. Then they cut the fruit open and gave it to us to drink. Immediately, we began to feel the results of the fruit; it completely satisfied our thirst and provided the electrolytes we needed. Fifteen minutes later, our headaches were gone and we were rejuvenated and ready to serve.

The Bible describes the fruit of the Spirit, but also fruit(s) of the flesh.

READ GALATIANS 5:19-21.

These things are obvious. The Spirit is not involved in these things. These are a direct result from our sinful nature (the flesh). When we feed the flesh, we will produce fruit. The fruits of the flesh are obviously not godly and will lead us down the road that leads to destruction (Matt. 7:13).

However, when we are in Christ, we have the Spirit who produces fruit in us and leads us down the path of life (Prov. 15:24). The evidence of the Spirit will also be obvious.

There is nothing more incredible than sweet fruit or a refreshing drink in times of physical thirst. Likewise, let's do what we can to feed our spirit and allow the Holy Spirit to produce the fruit of the Spirit in us to quench our spiritual thirst.

> *Look at your life. Do you produce fruit of the flesh more than the fruit of the Spirit? How can we produce fruit of the Spirit as opposed to the flesh?*

> *Pray that God will prepare your heart for this study and to walk in the Spirit.*

A WOMAN OF SAMARIA CAME TO DRAW WATER. "GIVE ME A DRINK,"
JESUS SAID TO HER, BECAUSE HIS DISCIPLES HAD GONE INTO TOWN
TO BUY FOOD. "HOW IS IT THAT YOU, A JEW, ASK FOR A DRINK FROM
ME, A SAMARITAN WOMAN?" SHE ASKED HIM. FOR JEWS DO NOT
ASSOCIATE WITH SAMARITANS. JESUS ANSWERED, "IF YOU KNEW
THE GIFT OF GOD, AND WHO IS SAYING TO YOU, 'GIVE ME A DRINK,'
YOU WOULD ASK HIM, AND HE WOULD GIVE YOU LIVING WATER."

JOHN 4:7-10

There was a woman who was embarrassed to be seen in public, so she went to draw water from a well in the middle of the day. She probably did this to avoid bumping into others. Why? Because she had been married five times and was currently living with someone who was not her husband. She likely wanted to avoid the drama. This story of the woman at the well is found in John 4.

READ THE ENTIRE PASSAGE—JOHN 4:1-26.

What jumps out to me is this: Jesus told her that the water she was drinking would leave her thirsty, but He had living water and that if she drank from it, she would never thirst again.

She had probably been trying to find love in her relationships with many different men. She had tried drinking the "water of this world" and it left her thirsty. But when she drank from the living water, her life was changed! The best way to cure your thirst is to drink from the right well. Jesus is the only water that will keep us satisfied.

Oftentimes people try to satisfy that thirst and yearning with other things. Some believe that if their life could just have some adjustments, then they will be satisfied, or have peace or joy. Some try to satisfy this emptiness with friends, or a relationship, while others turn to drinking, smoking, or even eating. I have also seen some try and fill that hole in their heart with money.

Nothing on this earth will ever fully satisfy our thirst. Only the living God can give you living water that will quench your soul's thirst. If you are longing for more, if you are searching, if you lack peace, if you have been chasing things of the world and realize nothing works, then look to Jesus. He is the living water your soul needs!

What things or people are you trying to fill your life with that are not worthy of your time? Are you finding your satisfaction in Jesus? If not, surrender to Him today.

BUT SOLID FOOD IS FOR THE MATURE—FOR THOSE WHOSE SENSES
HAVE BEEN TRAINED TO DISTINGUISH BETWEEN GOOD AND EVIL.

HEBREWS 5:14

My uncle is a police officer in south Louisiana. Several years ago he was called to a house in the middle of nowhere. People honestly didn't even know anyone lived in this remote area. As he drove up to the dilapidated mobile home with no electricity or water, he was not prepared for what he was about to witness.

He went inside to find a 15-year-old boy along with his 13-year-old brother both wearing diapers and nothing else. Their teeth were rotten and unformed, and their bodies severely under-developed. He found that these boys were still being bottle fed—still drinking milk and not eating solid food. Their parents, who were mentally ill, had not take proper care of them. As a result, they were severely malnourished. They acted like babies in many ways despite their age. It was the saddest thing my uncle has seen in over 30 years as a police officer.

What would happen if we only ate food that didn't have much nutritional value? For example, if you ate Skittles every day, how do you think your body would respond? On the other hand, if your diet consists of vegetables and foods high in protein with only occasional sweets, how do you think your body would respond? See where this is going? It's a choice. Choose to eat healthy food so you will be healthy or suffer the consequences. We need healthy spiritual food, or we won't make it. We must be mature and able to distinguish between good and evil, as Hebrews 5:14 reiterates.

> *Read 1 Corinthians 3:2-3 as well. What does the illustration of milk and solid food mean? How does it relate to where we are in our spiritual maturity?*

> *What disciplines or practices are you currently engaged in? Are these practices helping you grow to be more like Jesus? Why or why not?*

In this study we will discover the keys to living a healthy spiritual life. Some of those disciplines will be discussed and examined on a deep level. Some of my favorite disciplines are studying the Word, praying, fasting, ministry, solitude, worship, and community. These are essential to the growth of every believer.

Prepare yourself to dive into a feast of things that will feed your spirit. Begin by asking God to help you. Ask God to help you to live a life that is set apart and focused on serving Him. Ask for help to discipline yourself to seek His face.

SESSION 2

WORSHIP

VIDEO

GUIDE

Start by watching the video for Session 2. Brock begins with an illusion about choice, chance, and destiny. He shares specifically how worship is our destiny as believers and followers of Christ.

WE CANNOT FULLY AND COMPLETELY UNDERSTAND GOD. BROCK SHARES HOW THIS DRIVES US TO WORSHIP GOD. In the same way, Brock explains that he does tricks people sometimes cannot figure out. In the moment, when we can't understand something, there's space for mystery which should drive us to God and cause us to seek and trust Him. Even though we don't understand God fully, we should worship Him for who He is and what He has done.

> *According to Brock, what are some of the reasons why we should worship God? Are there any others you would add?*
>
> *What are some mysteries you cannot comprehend that cause you to worship God?*
>
> *What does worship look like in your day-to-day life?*
>
> *Discuss some ways you can grow in your worship of God and in disciplining yourself to worship Him in the future.*

As we worship, we remind ourselves of who God is. Our world should revolve around God. He is holy. He loves us and has forgiven us. He is always worthy of our worship.

OSWALD CHAMBERS ONCE SAID "WORSHIP IS GIVING GOD THE BEST THAT HE HAS GIVEN YOU."[1] This means we are not to give God the leftovers or simply a portion of what He has given us, but rather we should give Him the best that He has given us. When it comes to worship, this means giving our all. Worship is so much more than attending church on Sundays and Wednesdays. It means offering our entire lives to Him in worship.

> *What is worship? How do you worship?*

> *What would you do for the people you love? What would you give to them?*

How does this apply to your relationship with God? Think about the person you love most in the world. What would you do for that person? Maybe you would give him or her gifts, say nice things, or spend time with that person. Maybe you would serve that person by helping them clean or by preparing food for them.

There are many ways to show love, and each person shows love differently. But worship is the response we give God based on our love for Him. We worship Him because of who He is and what He has done. If you love Jesus and understand that He died and rose again so that you might have a relationship with God (1 Pet. 3:18), then you will naturally want to worship Him.

WHAT DOES GOD'S WORD SAY ABOUT WORSHIP AND HOW WE ARE TO WORSHIP?

- We are to offer our bodies to God as a living sacrifice (Rom. 12:1).
- We are to sing to the Lord (1 Chron. 16:23).
- We are to "ascribe to the LORD the glory of his name," and to bring Him an offering (1 Chron. 16:29).
- We are to tremble before Him (1 Chron. 16:30).
- We are to exalt the Lord (Ps. 99:5).
- We are to be thankful in your worship (Heb. 12:28).

Take a closer look at Psalm 100:

> *Let the whole earth shout triumphantly to God! Serve the LORD with gladness; come before him with joyful songs. Acknowledge that the LORD is God.*

> *He made us, and we are his—his people, the sheep of his pasture. Enter his gates with thanksgiving and his courts with praise. Give thanks to him and bless his name. For the LORD is good, and his faithful love endures forever; his faithfulness, through all generations.*

There are many verses that teach us about worship or how to worship, but I don't want you to get hung up on a rule or a specific act of worship. The main point is this: We are to give God the attention and ascribe to Him every bit of love and adoration He deserves.

WAYS TO WORSHIP

Perhaps the most obvious way to worship is through music. Every church plans music for its services. This music helps us corporately focus on and rejoice in God!

But, what if you can't sing? No problem. God isn't listening so much to your voice as He is to your heart. Focus intently on God and His character and allow your heart to praise Him. Let your heart be filled with joy and thanksgiving, then express that to God openly and honestly. Maybe you whisper the words of the songs being played or journal your words of praise and worship.

There are so many different ways to worship. You can worship through serving and giving. God longs for your heart to be fully devoted to Him, and for you to act on that devotion.

What are some specific ways you can "act on" your devotion to God?

MORE THAN MUSIC

All music is not worship to God just as all worship is not music. Music is a method of worship. It's a great method and a general way for us as a faith community to worship God as a group when we meet. But, some people have a tough time with worship. Maybe it's the song choice; maybe they don't give; maybe they don't offer their bodies as a living sacrifice. Maybe you have felt lost in worship and it just feels like you're going through the motions and following along with what the crowd is doing. Maybe you do not have a worshipful heart Monday through Saturday.

WORSHIP IS MORE THAN THE MUSIC— IT'S ABOUT YOUR HEART

If worship continues to be a struggle for you, then maybe there is a bigger issue. Maybe it's not about the music but about your relationship with the One being worshiped.

If worship does not come naturally to you, then search your heart and ask why? Does prayer come naturally? Does service come naturally?

Dig a little deeper and examine your heart. Do you have a truly life-changing relationship with the Father? If not, then think and pray about this.

SOMETHING WAS MISSING

Many people have been to church, or have even grown up in church but have never really found a real relationship with Jesus. This was the case for me—I grew up in church and my father was a pastor. I had walked the aisle a couple of times as a child and was even baptized, but when I was 15, I realized something was missing. I became sick of my sin and sinful lifestyle. I realized that even though I went to church, my life was just like everyone else at school. This realization was a wake-up call for me and I fully committed to follow Jesus. I surrendered my life to Jesus and watched Him begin to change me. My worship quickly changed. I now had a reason to worship. I now knew the One to worship. I now had the understanding and willingness to worship the God who had saved me and who had become my best friend.

Worship became joyful as I served the Lord in my church and community. Worship came naturally to me as I learned more about His character and His love for me. Singing the songs, even when I didn't care for the music style, was so much more joyful because I had finally met the One who loved me enough to die for me. I finally had a relationship with Him that was growing and intimate. That was a game changer.

THE FOCUS OF OUR WORSHIP—JESUS

If you do not have a real and growing relationship with Jesus, please know this: There is a God who loves you so much that He bankrupted heaven by sending Jesus, His only Son, to the earth to die for your sins. He lived perfectly and never sinned. Jesus was born of a virgin and was fully man and fully God. He came to pay the price for our sins.

You see, when God created the earth and put Adam and Eve in the garden of Eden, they eventually disobeyed God. They doubted God's Word and gave into the lie that He was holding out on them. Their sin was passed down from generation to generation. Every person born is under that curse of sin. Sin comes naturally for all of us and it separates us from God (Isa. 59:2; Rom. 3:23).

Jesus died on the cross and rose from the dead on the third day. This is the most important moment in history—He broke the power of sin and death. If we put our faith in the finished work of Jesus by surrendering to Him 100 percent, then because of His love and grace, He will save us from that sin and give us new life.

BAD NEWS, GOOD NEWS, AND OUR RESPONSE

There is bad news, good news, and our response. The bad news is we have sinned and are under the curse of sin, and sin brings death. The good news is Jesus loves us and paid the price for our sin. Our response to this gospel (good news) is to repent and believe—to turn toward Jesus and away from self (sin) and follow Him (Mark 1:15).

By understanding the weight of our sin and how much we have been forgiven, we can begin to worship. When we grasp how God has saved us from the slavery of sin and the consequences of sin (hell), then we can "enter his gates with thanksgiving and his courts with praise" (Ps. 100:4).

There are many ways to worship. But the first step is to be in a relationship with Jesus. Once you truly know Him you will find ways to worship without question. Need more motivation? Remember this: Jesus absolutely, most definitely loves you—without question. He loves you! He loves you! He doesn't care about who you are or what you have done wrong. His precious blood covers all sin and He loves you! Nothing can change that.

Let's worship Him!

Read Romans 12:1. How will you offer your body as a living sacrifice to God?

What have you learned about worship? What other questions do you have about worship?

Who or what is receiving your time and attention now that should not be? How will you give God your undivided attention?

There is a God who loves you so much that He bankrupted heaven by sending Jesus, His only Son, to the earth to die for your sins.

THEREFORE, BROTHERS AND SISTERS, IN VIEW OF THE MERCIES OF GOD, I URGE YOU TO PRESENT YOUR BODIES AS A LIVING SACRIFICE, HOLY AND PLEASING TO GOD; THIS IS YOUR TRUE WORSHIP. DO NOT BE CONFORMED TO THIS AGE, BUT BE TRANSFORMED BY THE RENEWING OF YOUR MIND, SO THAT YOU MAY DISCERN WHAT IS THE GOOD, PLEASING, AND PERFECT WILL OF GOD.

ROMANS 12:1-2

What is true worship? Webster's dictionary says to worship is "to honor with extravagant love and extreme submission."[2] This brings up the following questions. Is your love extravagant? Do you have extreme submission?

Maybe we need to start there. When we fall in extravagant love with Jesus, then we will begin to find true worship. When we are in extreme submission to God, then we will find that we are naturally ready to worship. Giving God honor with our extravagant love and extreme submission is true worship. It's much more than the feeling we get when our favorite song is played. Worship starts with falling in love with God. This requires knowing who God is and submitting more of your life to Him.

Looking back at today's Scripture, how would you define true worship?

What did Paul instruct believers to do in addition to offering their bodies as a living sacrifice?

True worship involves focusing on who God is as He reveals Himself in Scripture. Doing so leads us to live holy lives that are pleasing to the Lord. And living lives that are holy and pleasing to the Lord leads us to true worship.

How will you focus your heart and mind on God's goodness, glory, and greatness today? Tomorrow?

How might you offer more of yourself as a sacrifice of worship to God? What is one way you might worship God by obeying Him this week?

IN THE YEAR THAT KING UZZIAH DIED, I SAW THE LORD SEATED ON A HIGH
AND LOFTY THRONE, AND THE HEM OF HIS ROBE FILLED THE TEMPLE.
SERAPHIM WERE STANDING ABOVE HIM; THEY EACH HAD SIX WINGS: WITH
TWO THEY COVERED THEIR FACES, WITH TWO THEY COVERED THEIR FEET,
AND WITH TWO THEY FLEW. AND ONE CALLED TO ANOTHER: HOLY, HOLY,
HOLY IS THE LORD OF ARMIES; HIS GLORY FILLS THE WHOLE EARTH.

ISAIAH 6:1-3

I love great art. Performance art is my favorite. There are some people whose performances just capture me. I love feeling the moment of pure astonishment.

When I see something that creates this feeling of awe, everything stops. I escape reality and feel like I am caught up in another world where nothing is impossible. Before I get all artsy-weirdo on you, I want to bring it back down to earth. I know the feeling of great art, the emotion that can flood the heart. But those things are all temporary. What really overwhelms me is the holiness of God. When I see how great, how grand, and how incredible God is, I am truly overwhelmed. Why do I shudder? Because He is holy. He is beyond anything I have ever experienced in any earthly performance or adventure. God is truly exceptional.

> **When we worship, we worship a holy God. What is holiness?**

Holiness literally means *to be set apart*. It means to be without sin, or to be different from the world. God is the absolute perfect example of holiness. In the Book of Revelation, the angels cry out day and night to God saying "holy, holy, holy" (4:8). God is holy. Through faith in Christ, we are being made holy. This process is sanctification and it refers to the process of becoming more like Christ. When we worship, we can know that we are worshiping a worthy God because He is holy and has made us holy through the blood of Jesus.

When I look at my sin, I am disgusted. When I see how much God has forgiven me, I am blown away and driven to worship Him. Prayer and reading the Word are so vital because these practices expose my sin, reveal the idols in my heart, and remind me of God's promises. When we take these truths and promises to heart, worship will become a something we do every day.

> **Read John 3:30. How can you decrease today so that you might delight more in Christ? What might this look like?**

> **How might you make worship a part of your everyday life this week?**

I EXALT YOU, MY GOD THE KING, AND BLESS YOUR NAME
FOREVER AND EVER. I WILL BLESS YOU EVERY DAY; I WILL PRAISE
YOUR NAME FOREVER AND EVER. THE LORD IS GREAT AND IS
HIGHLY PRAISED; HIS GREATNESS IS UNSEARCHABLE.

PSALM 145:1-3

I saw a video one time about Michael Jackson. He was a worldwide superstar. He had millions of fans who were completely in awe of him. There are video clips of Michael walking onto the stage and people in the audience screaming his name.

Some of the fans would freak out and cry at the sight of Michael Jackson. This was a picture of false worship. Or maybe I should say it's a picture of true worship of a false god. Michael Jackson may have been a great singer or entertainer, but worship should be reserved for the only One worthy of worship. He was a mortal man with a sinful nature. Every superstar, no matter how great, will eventually fail and disappoint you because each has a sinful nature.

Reserve your worship for the One who is without sin. Worship the One who will never let you down. Worship the One who loves you more than you love Him. Worship the One who knows your name. If you go to a concert to see any famous musician, you will see thousands of fans adoring and watching his or her every move. Some people will hold up signs or lift their hands, or even sing every word of the songs. But there is one thing I can most certainly guarantee: The performer doesn't know who you are. That person doesn't know your name. That person doesn't care about you personally. That star on stage wants you in the audience because that's how they make money. Not to throw every performer under the bus, but it is essentially impossible for them to know the names or stories of the thousands of people in their audience. Remember that God knows your name. He knows your story. He knows your past, and He knows your future. He is worthy to be praised. He is worthy of worship.

Have you caught yourself worshiping something unworthy?

How does God's personal care and knowledge of you change your attitude about Him? How should knowing this change the way you live?

How does the way God knows and loves you influence the way you worship Him?

BECAUSE OF THE LORD'S FAITHFUL LOVE WE DO NOT PERISH, FOR HIS MERCIES NEVER END. THEY ARE NEW EVERY MORNING; GREAT IS YOUR FAITHFULNESS! I SAY, "THE LORD IS MY PORTION, THEREFORE I WILL PUT MY HOPE IN HIM."

LAMENTATIONS 3:22-24

Who is worship for?

I live in Nashville, so when I was writing this book I decided to go have a conversation with my friend Phil Joel (formerly of the Newsboys, currently leader of the band Zealand). As a musician who has written dozens of worship songs and taught on worship, I wanted to get his thoughts on worship. As we sat on his front porch, this is the gist of what he shared, although I'm paraphrasing: "We think worship is for God, but He doesn't need to be worshiped in order to be happy and full. He already knows the things we sing to Him or say to Him. He is God."

But, we also need to worship God because it's for us. The purpose of worship can be settled on this simple truth: It's a reminder for us of how great He is and how much we need Him. Worship reminds us who God is. It reminds us that He is good. It reminds us of what He has already done. And it reminds us of His holiness.

Worship reminds us of who God is and what He has done. Sometimes we see God as some attention hungry, old white-haired judge sitting on a throne waiting for us to mess up. We think God simply wants and needs us to worship Him. This is so not true. God is worthy of our worship, but He needs nothing. He created us, but worshiping Him is more than our obligation. It brings us to a place of understanding His character so that we love Him more. Don't get me wrong, God loves when His children worship Him. Maybe it's like when parents hear their child say *I love you*. God doesn't need that acknowledgment to be who He is, but He loves and longs for us to love and worship Him.

READ LAMENTATIONS 3:22-24.

Do you need a reminder of who God is and how much He loves you?

What are some examples of spiritual food? How will you fill your life with things of God and the Spirit this week?

Does it surprise you that worshiping God is for us and for Him? Why or why not?

I WILL BLESS THE LORD AT ALL TIMES; HIS PRAISE WILL ALWAYS BE ON MY LIPS.
I WILL BOAST IN THE LORD; THE HUMBLE WILL HEAR AND BE GLAD. PROCLAIM
THE LORD'S GREATNESS WITH ME; LET US EXALT HIS NAME TOGETHER.

PSALM 34:1-3

When and where should we worship?

I am a magician, or if that term bothers you, I am an illusionist. Unlike what some may want to believe, it is hard work. It's not as easy as waving a wand. Much physical dexterity is necessary. I spend hours training my muscles to accomplish the sleight of hand required to do card tricks or make coins "disappear." The reality is that if I don't practice, then I get sloppy. If I don't spend hours working on my effects, then I can't perform or create anything of beauty on stage or on camera. I have no option, I must find time to practice.

Most people think of worship as something that happens at church on Sundays. The truth is, we can worship through music at church or just about anywhere. Finding moments to take advantage of the time during our busy schedules is essential to keeping the Spirit fed and the flesh starved.

Think of it as practicing for your big moment on stage or the field. Athletes and musicians will find ways to practice before their big moment. If there is no practice, then they will get rusty, and eventually be unprepared to take the stage or the field.

Let's not wait for Sunday morning, with the lighting just so, and the band sounding perfect, before we worship.

Music is a wonderful way to connect with God. It's a great way to communicate what's in your heart. Music is a method. You can connect with God even if there is no music playing. Turn your heart toward God and prayerfully worship anywhere and anytime.

Our worship is both individual and corporate. But don't be confused, even our corporate worship at church is individual worship. However, we need the freedom to worship anywhere. Put in some headphones and see how your heart can turn to God and give Him praise, thanksgiving, or adoration. Try this on the bus, at work, or while shopping.

READ PSALM 34:1-8.

> *What are some practical ways you can worship God individually? List a few ways you will take refuge in Him this week.*

WHEN I KEPT SILENT, MY BONES BECAME BRITTLE FROM MY GROANING ALL DAY LONG. FOR DAY AND NIGHT YOUR HAND WAS HEAVY ON ME; MY STRENGTH WAS DRAINED AS IN THE SUMMER'S HEAT. THEN I ACKNOWLEDGED MY SIN TO YOU AND DID NOT CONCEAL MY INIQUITY. I SAID, "I WILL CONFESS MY TRANSGRESSIONS TO THE LORD," AND YOU FORGAVE THE GUILT OF MY SIN.

PSALM 32:3-5

READ PSALM 51.

In Psalm 51, we see David in the moments after he was caught in adultery and murder. He realized his sin and turned in repentance. Even as a home-wrecking, adulterous murderer, David found forgiveness and a reason to worship God. The reason? His forgiveness. That forgiveness motivated him to worship.

What did David ask from God? What did David praise God for?

As verse 14 reiterates, it's God's righteousness that allows us to worship Him. Not because we are worthy, but because of who God is. He has saved us from sin. He has saved us and forgiven us of our sin. That leads us to worship.

David was in trouble. He refused to confess his sin or admit wrongdoing and humble himself before the Lord. The result was pain and anguish. However, there is freedom in confessing our sins. That freedom leads us to worship. In freedom we see who the Savior is. Free people can worship because we are free to worship. When it's difficult to worship, or when you can't find motivation to worship, examine your heart and ask God to reveal sin. If you find sin or anything close to rebellion, then the answer is to immediately confess it as sin. Go to God and admit the shortcoming or utter failure and watch what happens. He will flood you with His grace. The blood of Christ will erase the sin and you will realize you are clean. You are free. The guilt is gone. All shame is gone. All sin is forgotten. He refuses to count your sins against you.

How sinful was David? He was a murderer and an adulterer. He was a liar and abused his power. He was at his lowest point, yet God forgave him without question. If God forgave a murdering adulterer like David, then surely He can forgive you and me. Our God is good and forgiving. He is worthy of all the worship our hearts have to give.

How could David worship God even after committing murder? How might you follow David's example?

SESSION 3

SCRIPTURE

Begin by watching the video for Session 3. It starts with an illusion with a sword and Brock introduces the importance of Scripture. Hebrews 4:12 says "the word of God is living and effective and sharper than any double-edged sword."

THE WORD OF GOD IS ALIVE AND ACTIVE. IT IS POWERFUL. BROCK SHARES A STORY ABOUT BELIEVERS IN NORTH KOREA AND THE PERSECUTION THEY FACE DAILY BECAUSE OF THE GOSPEL.

Do you really believe that the Word of God is living and active? Are you desperate to know God's Word?

How will you value God's Word and believe in the power of His Word this week?

Brock shares how the Bible is our source for faith and practice—it provides the foundation both for what we believe and how we are to live. He shares how when we spend time in God's Word, then we'll feast on it and grow in our desire for it. The Word of God is our secret weapon. It gives us the ability to understand truth. The flesh and world will lie to us, but God's Word is the truth we need to flood our minds with as we walk with Christ.

How well do you know the Word of God?

What can we avoid by staying in the Word of God?

How can we know the will of God?

Brock challenges us to spend time in God's Word. Make a plan for how and when specifically you will designate time to read, study, dwell on, and memorize God's Word this week.

THERE IS A GAME THAT SCHOOLS PLAY IN NORTH KOREA. THE GAME IS EXPLAINED TO THE CHILDREN AT SCHOOL EACH YEAR. They are told that there is a secret book that their parents have hidden at their house. If you can find the secret book, then you win a prize. What the kids don't realize is that the secret book they are talking about is the Bible. They also don't realize that the prize they get is imprisonment. If they find the secret hidden book and take it to the school, they and their family are taken away and put into torture camps and executed.

People risk their lives every day as they smuggle Bibles into countries that have outlawed God's Word. If they are caught, they will likely never see their families again.

Why would people risk their lives to read the Bible? Why would people risk everything to smuggle a Bible into another country? These people know, on a personal level, the life transforming power of God's Word. They know the hope and the power Scripture holds. It is worth dying for. They know that the Word of God is like a secret weapon. It has the ability to change a culture, community, or a nation. The Word of God is alive and sharper than a double-edged sword (Heb. 4:13). It is powerful and has the ability to change your life. That's why people throughout history have risked their lives to make the Bible accessible to other people.

William Tyndale translated the Scriptures into English in the 1500s, but he paid a high price. Tyndale had to leave England and hide in Germany for fear of his life as he translated the Bible into the common language of his people. It was illegal to have a Bible in English, but Tyndale understood that people needed access to the Scriptures without having to go to a priest in the Catholic church. As Tyndale translated the New Testament and then the Old Testament, he was always looking over his shoulder. This went on for years until one day a man by the name of Henry Phillips befriended him and betrayed him. Tyndale was arrested and taken back to England where they tied a rope around his neck and built a large fire underneath his gallows and had him executed. His last words were a prayer, "Lord, open the eyes of the king of England!" [1]

THE MOST IMPORTANT BOOK OF ALL TIME— THE BIBLE

There has been so much blood spilled for us to have God's Word today. Some people think it's just another old book. Actually, it's a collection of 66 books written by 40 authors on three continents in three languages. Most of the New Testament was written by eyewitnesses of Jesus' resurrection in front of other eyewitnesses. This book has stood the test of time. It has weathered every accusation, trial, and scrutiny, and yet it still stands as the most important book of all time.

The words on its pages were breathed out by God (2 Tim. 3:16-17) for us to read. God literally spoke through those writing it down so that we can have the message and story that God wants us to hear. It is impossible to overvalue this book. The Scriptures are to be applied to our lives daily and thoroughly. We should absorb them and allow them to make us more like Jesus.

How can your group make Scripture a greater part of your lives? Take time to thank God for His Word and carve out time this week to listen to His voice.

Read James 1:2-4. How does the testing of our faith produce endurance? What can we learn from Tyndale's life and the price he paid to follow Christ?

Some of my favorite verses are:

- *Now I lay me down to sleep, I pray the Lord my soul to keep . . .*
- *God helps those who help themselves.*
- *God grant me the serenity to accept the things I cannot change . . .*

Did you fall for any of those? These sayings are not found in Scripture. They may sound good, but they are not God's Word. I don't need pithy sayings. I want God's Word in me. I don't want something that merely sounds good. I want truth. I want to feast on the words of my heavenly Father. We can rest assured that the Scripture we have is the Word of God.

Do we truly believe that the Bible is the source of our faith and practice?

How should knowing that the Bible is God-breathed change the way we read it?

MAKING THE BIBLE A PRIORITY

I think many people who go to church do not actually believe that the Bible is the Word of God that can change their lives. I have found that many church-goers are biblically illiterate—they don't really know the Bible they claim as God's Word. In my years of ministry I have noticed that most people cannot quote more than two or three Bible verses. Even in the Bible Belt where it's common to have churches on every corner, there is still a huge lack of knowledge about the Bible.

Don't mishear me, Scripture memory is not a requirement to be loved by God, but if you are following Jesus and seeking Him, you will be in His Word. And if you spend time in the Word, it will begin to stick. Eventually you will be able to quote it from memory.

You might be thinking that you have a bad memory. Consider this, how many song lyrics or movie lines can you quote? Whatever you spend time around, you will know.

Many people don't know the will of God because they don't know the Word of God. Many people don't know God personally because they don't know the Word of God. You can actually get to know God intimately by spending time in His Word. He will reveal His character, His heart, His way, His love, and His plan for your life and the world through His holy Word.

Dr. Joan Menninger said that "Scientists estimate that we remember only 1 out of 100 pieces (of information) we receive." [2] Therefore, we need to memorize as much as we can in order to recall it when we need it.

The secret weapon is that the Bible is full of truth. That truth will give you wisdom and knowledge that can prevent sin from winning. When the attacks come, you always have the secret weapon of memorized Scripture to combat it. We are in a spiritual battle; the enemy wants to destroy us. We have the Word as our secret weapon.

Ephesians 6:10 tells us to be strong in the Lord and in His mighty power and to put on the full armor of God — which is the Word of God.

How can we memorize Scripture? By spending time around it. If you are in it, then it will stick. When we are in the Word we will experience the sweet presence of Jesus. What a gift! We can be in the presence of God as He reveals His Word to us. Wow!

In the front of his Bible, D.L. Moody wrote, "This book will keep you from sin or sin will keep you from this book." [3]

I was speaking at a Christian conference in the Midwest many years ago and I was teaching on the subject of worship. Afterward, a group of people surrounded me. They were trying to convince me that you do not need to read Scripture to know God. They were screaming at me saying, "just because I read Shakespeare doesn't mean I can know Shakespeare!" They are right about that part. Shakespeare is dead.

God is alive and His Word is alive.

> In the beginning was the Word, and the Word was with God, and the Word was God. —John 1:1

> The Word became flesh and dwelt among us. We observed his glory, the glory as the one and only Son from the Father, full of grace and truth. —John 1:14

Jesus can be known by reading the Bible. Knowing the Word will feed your spirit and will help you flourish. The best way to feed the Spirit and starve the flesh is by filling up on the Word of God and allowing it to be the nourishment for our spirit.

> . . . because the one who sows to his flesh will reap destruction from the flesh, but the one who sows to the Spirit will reap eternal life from the Spirit. —Galatians 6:8 (ESV)

Our choice is simple—we can do that which leads to corruption or that which leads to eternal life. We can feed the flesh or the Spirit. It is a life or death choice—the one we feed will grow and the stakes could not be higher.

On Robert Noland's blog, The Knight's Code, he says: "God's Word, coupled with the power of the Holy Spirit in us, is a powerful weapon to defeat sin, defend our faith, and advance the Kingdom in us, to lead us to love God more than our own mess." [4]

No wonder that in our very busy lives the enemy works so hard to convince us we don't have time or that the Bible is not relevant to our struggles.

Jesus said in John 17:17: "Sanctify them by the truth; your word is truth."

God's Word has a way for you to avoid the pitfall of sin. Look what the author of Psalm 119 says:

> *How can a young man keep his way pure? By keeping your word. I have sought you with all my heart; don't let me wander from your commands. I have treasured your word in my heart so that I may not sin against you. —Psalm 119:9-11*

The Word of God is fascinating! It is full of historical stories of real people with real lives doing extraordinary things. It's full of stories of romance, war, betrayal, victory, and miracles. There is wisdom and truth that can be applied to our daily lives right now—today. When we study the Bible, we find answers to our deepest questions and direction in our most pressing problems. Scripture not only equips us to think clearly, but also to live selflessly. As you study the Bible more, you will find yourself better equipped to love and serve the people around you. God's Word opens our eyes to God's glory and it opens our hearts to the people around us. If you are not consistently seeking God in His Word, you are missing out. There is an adventure awaiting you each day where you can hear God's voice and watch Him confirm and reveal His will. He will guide you through the day and you will see blessings, peace, and His presence as you walk through good times and bad. The Word of God is powerful, active, and alive. Let's sink our teeth into the Word of God and let it feed us, sustain us, and transform us. Let's feed the Spirit. Let's feed the dog.

FOR THE WORD OF GOD IS LIVING AND EFFECTIVE AND SHARPER
THAN ANY DOUBLE-EDGED SWORD, PENETRATING AS FAR AS THE
SEPARATION OF SOUL AND SPIRIT, JOINTS AND MARROW. IT IS ABLE
TO JUDGE THE THOUGHTS AND INTENTIONS OF THE HEART.

HEBREWS 4:12

There is a book called *Expert at the Card Table* by S.W. Erdnase. It's widely considered by illusionists to be one of the most important books on card tricks. Illusionists have studied this book for over 100 years.

The true masters of card effects have poured over this book's pages. But here is the problem: we don't really know who wrote it. The author has never been discovered in history or in other books. None of the famous or influential magicians of that era mentioned him. No one has seen him or met him. In fact, if you look up the name Erdnase, you will have trouble finding anyone with that last name. So, who was he? How can we be sure that someone by the name of S.W. Erdnase even wrote this book? The book is a goldmine of skills and techniques, and yet we may never know the true identity of the person who wrote it. However, we actually do know the authors of the Bible. For example, we know who wrote the Gospel of Luke and the Book of Acts. Luke was a physician. He carefully studied the accounts of what happened in the life of Jesus and the apostles, and he was careful to get the details right. We can trust what Luke says because we know who he was and his writing matches other sources. The Bible is the most important book of all time. It can be trusted. Its power continues to be proven throughout history.

Unlike Erdnase, the authors of the Bible have credibility and trusted character. Why does this matter? Because the Bible is no ordinary book. It is God's Word and it was written by eyewitnesses in front of eyewitnesses. The Bible's most important claims, like the resurrection of Jesus, can be verified. When your flesh tries to convince you that the Bible is just an old book, remember that Scripture is inspired by God—He used specific people who He called to write the truth we find on its pages.

So, let's read the Word with confidence. Let's read the Bible and allow it to change us.

Have you ever been tempted to believe that the Bible can't be trusted? How did you overcome this temptation?

How will you deepen your trust in God and in His Word this week?

THE ONE WHO HAS MY COMMANDS AND KEEPS THEM IS THE ONE WHO
LOVES ME. AND THE ONE WHO LOVES ME WILL BE LOVED BY MY FATHER.
I ALSO WILL LOVE HIM AND WILL REVEAL MYSELF TO HIM." JUDAS (NOT
ISCARIOT) SAID TO HIM, "LORD, HOW IS IT YOU'RE GOING TO REVEAL
YOURSELF TO US AND NOT TO THE WORLD?" JESUS ANSWERED, "IF
ANYONE LOVES ME, HE WILL KEEP MY WORD. MY FATHER WILL LOVE
HIM, AND WE WILL COME TO HIM AND MAKE OUR HOME WITH HIM.

JOHN 14:21-23

Why should we know the Word of God?

So that we can walk in obedience. Obedience does not come naturally to anyone. We all have the tendency to rebel from birth. Scripture, however, is clear—God calls us to obey Him. But we have a problem.

In Exodus 24:7 we see God making the first covenant with His people. The response from God's people was, "We will do and obey all that the LORD has commanded." His people collectively agreed to do all God had spoken and be completely obedient to Him. Their response, though they probably were a little too confident in their ability to obey, reflected their humble and repentant hearts. If we want to be close to God, we must be obedient. But how can we be obedient outside of knowing, understanding, and applying the Word of God? The Word shows us His way and His will. We won't submit to God if we don't study His Word.

It really all comes down to this: Do we really love God? If we love Him, then we will obey Him. If we love Him, then we will want to feast on Scripture. It really is that simple.

How will you dwell on God's commands this week?

What specific commands are you struggling the most to obey?

Take some time to pray for the strength to be obedient to God in these areas of your life. Allow the Word to guide you to live in obedience to God's commands.

. . . BUT WHENEVER A PERSON TURNS TO THE LORD, THE VEIL IS REMOVED.

2 CORINTHIANS 3:16

I was recently in New York City where I decided to go watch a famous illusionist from the United Kingdom who specializes in illusion techniques based on psychology. He asked the audience to look for a gorilla on stage as he placed a banana on a lamp stand.

After a few minutes he pointed to the stand only to find the banana was gone. So he put out another banana. Later I realized the banana was gone yet again. I never saw the gorilla. My friend sitting next to me saw it both times but most of the audience missed it. How is it possible to be intently watching the stage and yet miss a person, wearing a giant gorilla suit, walk out and take the banana? The answer is quite simple: It's because of our cognitive blind spots. A cognitive blind spot hinders us from seeing the whole picture. Our brain can only handle a certain amount of info at a time. It has a limited amount of bandwidth and therefore misses some things.

The spiritual life also has blind spots. We can be blind to the obvious sin in our lives and not even realize it. It may be the way we are acting toward someone, or believing something false, but we all have moments of blindness.

Before we come to Christ, we are all spiritually blind. We cannot see or understand the truth.

According to Paul, Satan has "blinded the minds of the unbelievers to keep them from seeing the light of the gospel of the glory of Christ, who is the image of God" (2 Cor. 4:4).

READ 2 CORINTHIANS 3:16 AGAIN.

We are spiritually blind until we turn to the Lord and the veil is removed.

So, how do we remove blind spots? By reading and understanding the Word of God. Read it, study it, and meditate on it. The Word is a light that will remove blind spots. Anything lurking in the shadows of our hearts will be exposed.

How can we help others come to faith in Christ and no longer live in blindness?

Paul answers that in Romans 10:17 when he explains that faith comes by hearing. And the only way for people to hear the gospel is for someone to speak it to them. Romans 10:14 says "how can they hear without a preacher?"

Who do you need to share truth from God's Word with this week? Why can it be challenging to share our faith?

AND HE SAID, 'THE GOD OF OUR ANCESTORS HAS APPOINTED YOU
TO KNOW HIS WILL, TO SEE THE RIGHTEOUS ONE, AND TO HEAR
THE WORDS FROM HIS MOUTH, SINCE YOU WILL BE A WITNESS FOR
HIM TO ALL PEOPLE OF WHAT YOU HAVE SEEN AND HEARD.

ACTS 22:14-15

My friend, Jason, is a musician. He played in a band that toured the world for about 15 years. He currently spends time in a studio mastering music for other artists' records. He listens for small imperfections and makes adjustments to make the music sound better for the listener.

Jason has an ear like no one I have ever known. He can hear in ways most humans cannot; he hears everything. You can take a coin out of your pocket and drop it on the floor and he can tell you what type of coin hit the floor. He hears with precision.

What if I told you that you could have spiritual ears that hear with the same sort of precision? When we listen to the Word of God, we are hearing God's voice. God uses the Word to speak with precision to His children. When we hear the Word of God whispered in our minds, we can more clearly hear God's direction, His will, and His answer. This doesn't happen overnight, it takes time. You must learn to read the Bible in context so that you can understand spiritual truth the way God wants you to.

You don't have to be an expert, but you do need to put the time in reading and learning what the Scriptures are telling you.

Have you come to a crossroads in life where you wish you knew the answer? Have you found yourself wondering what was best in a decision you were trying to make? Have you ever wished that you could just hear the answer so you know what to do?

The more you understand the Bible, the more equipped you will be to find the answers to these types of questions. God's Word equips us with the wisdom and direction we need to do God's will and live for His glory.

READ ACTS 22:14-15.

> *What did Ananias say to Paul about God's will? How can you, like Paul, know God's will?*

> *How will you study, rest in, and live out God's will for you this week?*

YOUR WORD IS A LAMP FOR MY FEET AND A LIGHT ON MY PATH.

PSALM 119:105

I had a conversation with someone recently who was in a serious relationship with her boyfriend. She was about to graduate from college and was hoping to be engaged soon.

She seemed genuinely excited about this guy and the possibility of marriage. I had never met her boyfriend and I respect her, so I asked her about his relationship with the Lord. I asked her if he reads and talks about the Bible. I asked her if he talks openly about his relationship with Christ. Her answers were vague. She couldn't remember having many conversations with him about Christ or the Bible. I suggested she might want to consider pumping the brakes on this relationship. If we are committed to following Christ, then we will be in the Word. If we are in the Word, then it will be a part of our conversations with close friends and family, and especially other believers.

> *How has God been speaking to you lately through His Word? How has the Bible shaped the way you think and live?*

Maybe you don't know how to answer these questions because you are not very familiar with Scripture. My challenge to you is to get in God's Word and feast on it. Consider keeping a Bible near your bed. Read it before you get going each day. List some verses on notecards and post them by your mirror and read them while you brush your teeth.

Put the Bible app on your smartphone, and set up alerts and reminders to read it every day. Find a Bible plan to read the Scriptures. Use little moments of downtime during the day to open the Bible or a Bible app on your phone and read a little bit at a time. Designate a specific time each day when you will shut off your phone for the purpose of dwelling on God's Word.

> *As you have been reading God's Word this week, what has stood out to you? Has God's Word challenged how you have been living? How so?*

Spend some time in prayer, asking God to help you be committed to studying and applying the truth of His Word in the weeks and months to come.

FOR THOSE WHO LIVE ACCORDING TO THE FLESH HAVE THEIR MINDS SET
ON THE THINGS OF THE FLESH, BUT THOSE WHO LIVE ACCORDING TO THE
SPIRIT HAVE THEIR MINDS SET ON THE THINGS OF THE SPIRIT. NOW THE
MIND-SET OF THE FLESH IS DEATH, BUT THE MIND-SET OF THE SPIRIT IS LIFE
AND PEACE. THE MIND-SET OF THE FLESH IS HOSTILE TO GOD BECAUSE
IT DOES NOT SUBMIT TO GOD'S LAW. INDEED, IT IS UNABLE TO DO SO.

ROMANS 8:5-7

The only way that you will grow in Christ is if you set your mind on it. You must get serious. This is your moment. Decide to set your mind on feeding your spirit and make it happen.

Remember the illustration with two dogs—the one we feed will grow the biggest. If we feed our minds the Word of God, then we will grow the spirit and starve the flesh. Simple, right?

READ ROMANS 8:5-7 AGAIN.

I want to please God. I want to be fully submissive to Him but according to Paul, I can't (v. 7), at least not on my own. I need God's help. I need to cry out to Him for the strength necessary to set my mind on the Word of God.

Each day we need ask God to help us set our minds on the truth of the gospel.

> *What else can we set our minds on? What does Paul say we should set our minds on (see Phil. 4:8)?*

READ COLOSSIANS 3:1-2.

> *How will you make time and space for setting your mind on "things above" this week?*

The discipline of reading and setting your mind on God's Word will change your life. The more you feed on the truth, promises, and hope found in Scripture, the more you will grow to be like Christ. Take some time now to pray that God would help you clear your mind of all the pressures, temptations, and distractions in your life. Focus on Him and the truth of His Word. Ask Him to help you prioritize time in His Word every day this week.

SESSION 4 ————

PRAYER

Start by watching the video for Session 4. It begins with an illusion and Brock explains how prayer is not a magic charm. He shares how our prayers should be aligned with God's will.

PRAYER IS NOT ABOUT GETTING SOMETHING, BUT ABOUT SPENDING TIME WITH GOD.

> *Do you think about prayer as talking with God or do you view it as something more complex?*

> *When should we pray? Why should we pray?*

Brock shares Ephesians 6:18 which reminds us we are to "pray at all times" and how our attitude should be prayerful throughout the day.

> *What does Brock share as a reason our lives may be powerless? How can we walk in a spirit of prayer?*

> *How does your perspective on prayer need to change?*

> *Do you view prayer as fellowship and conversation with God, or is it intimidating for you to pray?*

Remember that we can go to God in prayer. He loves us and listens to us. Prayer is a key component of the spiritual disciplines that will help us to feed the Spirit rather than the flesh. We'll explore this more in this session. Pray that God would prepare your heart and mind for what He has to teach you this week.

ONE DAY I CAME HOME TO FIND I HAD BEEN ROBBED. I lost all my gear for my show including a trailer full of illusion props, sound equipment, and lighting. I was devastated. I knew God had called me to do ministry using illusions in order to draw crowds, but I was now left with nothing. How was I supposed to continue?

My wife and I began to pray specifically and according to God's will. In a few months, God began supplying our needs. We had four pages in a notebook where we had specific prayer needs and saw specific answers to those prayers. Line by line, it is filled with miraculous answers to the prayers. God provided so that our ministry could continue. This wasn't something He owed us. Through this trial, and through prayer, God was teaching us to depend on Him.

This trial taught us to pray specifically. As we were rebuilding, we realized we needed a sound system for our show. We prayed and donations began coming in. When we went to make the purchase, we saw that a new system had been released. It cost 200 dollars more than we budgeted. We were willing to settle for the cheaper system but that night as we prayed, God answered. Someone we had not met walked up to us and handed us an envelope. Inside was 200 dollars. God answered our prayers.

It was amazing to see God sustaining us and providing for us. We, along with many other friends and family, were praying and seeking to submit ourselves to God's will. As we prayed, God began to change us in the process. The entire experience, although traumatic at first, became a catalyst for God to change me so I would be ready for the next stage of ministry.

But, God doesn't answer every prayer, at least not in the way we want. In fact, if He gave us everything we asked for, then we would be a mess. We would be a wreck! I sometimes thank God for unanswered prayers. If I had gotten every prayer answered my way, I would have married the wrong person, worked the wrong job, found the wrong friends, and it continues.

> *If you asked people at your school or in your neighborhood to define prayer, what do you think they would say?*

FIRST, LET'S TALK ABOUT WHAT PRAYER IS NOT.

Prayer is not a spiritual gift that is reserved for those who are really good at it. When we need someone to pray before an event or meal, who do we ask? The tendency is to look for the person who seems most qualified to pray, perhaps a pastor or ministry leader. We assume having the pastor pray means God will hear because the pastor is a professional. This is not true. Anyone who is a child of God has access to God through prayer and God listens to His children when they pray. No matter your age, background, or experience, God invites you to speak to Him through prayer.

Prayer is not a magic charm. We sometimes treat prayer like it's a secret formula to get something from God. Some people think they can get stuff from God by saying the right prayers. Some people think they can avoid difficult or unfortunate circumstances by praying the right way. Prayer is not a magic charm that makes bad things go away.

Prayer is not a performance. Some people think prayer requires knowing fancy words. Some are afraid of praying in public for fear of not being able to say a "good prayer." I have a friend who is scared to death that he will be called on to pray in front of a group. Prayer is not a performance. We don't pray to win anyone's approval.

Prayer is not a secret formula. I had a friend tell me about this special prayer that was found in the Old Testament. She said that if you pray it word-for-word everyday then God will bless you and give you things. The prayer is 32 words, one sentence. God is not sitting around waiting for someone to discover this secret and then repeat it every day for a few weeks before He finally blesses His children.

What is prayer? What does it look like to pray according to God's will?

Simply put, prayer is conversation between you and God. Prayer happens when a child of God talks to his or her heavenly Father. Think of it this way. You probably have someone in your life who you love very much. Maybe a parent, a brother or sister, or maybe even a friend. It's easy to talk to that person and spend time with that person. Prayer is similar. We spend time talking and listening to Jesus in His Word.

In 2017, a teenage boy was with his friends at the lunch room at his high school in Wisconsin. As they were laughing and joking around, he noticed a guy across the table turning blue in the face and holding his neck. He quickly realized the boy was choking on a cheese curd. The boy acted by giving his friend the Heimlich maneuver and saving his life. The entire thing was caught on camera and ended up on national news. These boys are friends, but after this lifesaving event, I am sure they are now closer. One boy is a hero and the other is probably just so thankful to be alive. If the boy who was choking never talked to the hero, then it would be clear that he was probably not grateful. Even more importantly, it would be clear they do not have a real relationship. Similarly, Jesus is our hero if we have truly been saved by Him. We should continue in our relationship with Him by spending time with Him. He is our friend, our advocate, our hero, and our Father.

When should we pray? Why?

Any time we have opportunity. We should also make prayer a part of our daily schedule.

"Devote yourselves to prayer; stay alert in it with thanksgiving." –Colossians 4:2

It should be a priority in our lives. Jesus prayed early and often. If Jesus needed to retreat often to pray, then how do we expect to make it without doing the same?

We should find a time that works for us to get still so we can pray and listen to the voice of God.

How should we pray? What sorts of things should we pray about?

READ ROMANS 8:15.

You did not receive a spirit of slavery to fall back into fear. Instead, you received the Spirit of adoption, by whom we cry out, "Abba, Father!"

Because we have been adopted into God's family, we can go to Him knowing He is our Father. We approach God as "our Father." He is not just my Father, He is your Father. He is our Father. The Father listens to His children.

When Jesus was asked how to pray, He responded with this in Matthew 6:5-8.

Whenever you pray, you must not be like the hypocrites, because they love to pray standing in the synagogues and on the street corners to be seen by people. Truly I tell you, they have their reward. But when you pray, go into your private room, shut your door, and pray to your Father who is in secret. And your Father who sees in secret will reward you. When you pray, don't babble like the Gentiles, since they imagine they'll be heard for their many words. Don't be like them, because your Father knows the things you need before you ask him.

Don't waste your words trying to show off how great you are or how much you know. God wants us to pray honestly and intimately. We don't need to use big fancy words. Pray from your heart. A model of prayer is the Lord's Prayer in Matthew 6:9-13. Read the Lord's Prayer and see how you can use this as a model to pray from your heart with your specific needs.

In the Lord's Prayer, Jesus lays out five essential aspects that should shape and guide our prayers:

- praise
- thanksgiving
- confession
- petition
- intercession

When we pray, it is always good to praise God. Tell Him how great He is. The goal is not to inform God of anything, God already knows He is great. We praise Him in order to draw nearer to Him—to remind ourselves of His greatness so that we might center our lives on Him.

Read Psalm 66:18. What hinders our prayers?

We should thank Him for who He is and for what He has done. We should confess our sin. Our prayers may be hindered if we have unconfessed sin.

When we pray, we can petition God. We can ask Him for things according to His will. Praying according to God's will is the best way to pray.

READ 1 JOHN 5:14-15.

> *What is promised to those who pray according to God's will? How can you know God's will?*

God's will is most clearly revealed to us in His Word. When we pray in accord with the teaching of His Word, we can be confident that He hears us. We should also pray for others. Intercession is about standing in the gap. It's praying on the behalf of others. There are those who do not know Jesus and they need our prayers. We should be praying for the people in our community, including students at our schools, friends in our neighborhoods, and family members who don't know Jesus. Pray for them consistently.

> *Who is someone in your life who you can be praying for every day?*

I like to set up alerts on my phone to remind myself to pray. There is even an app I have used called Prayer Notebook. It reminds me to pray for my friends who do not know Christ.

Don't give into the lie that prayer is a waste of time. I have a friend who spent a few months praying for her family member who was dying of cancer. She said that if God doesn't heal him, then all that prayer was a waste of time. She doesn't understand prayer. Prayer is a privilege, an opportunity, and a responsibility. We have been granted the ability to talk to the Creator of the universe. The Father of all allows us to approach Him. And prayer changes us!

> *Pray at all times in the Spirit with every prayer and request, and stay alert with all perseverance and intercession for all the saints. —Ephesians 6:18*

We should pray without ceasing. But, so many people who go to church do not pray and prayer-less Christianity is the evidence of counterfeit Christianity. If your life is powerless then it might be because it's prayer-less. We need to pray more than just before a test or at dinner time. We need an attitude of prayer that takes us through the day so we can continue to feed the Spirit. Remember, we don't pray to get what we want from God, we pray to draw close to Him. Getting an answer from God is not our biggest need. Spending time with the Father is our biggest need.

It's not the amount of time as much as it is the subject. Yes, we should spend time with God whenever possible, but don't get overwhelmed. A little bit of time a few times throughout the day is great and 15 minutes every morning is better than nothing at all. It's easy if you think about it. If you truly love someone, you will want to spend time with him or her. Take some time now to ask yourself, "how can I find a time to pray each day? How can I make sure I spend time in fellowship with my heavenly Father?"

By praying each day, you will see your spiritual life come alive and flourish. You will be amazed at the life you will experience just by making the discipline of prayer a daily habit.

1 DEVOTION
STUDY DAY ONE

"THIS, THEN, IS HOW YOU SHOULD PRAY: "'OUR FATHER IN HEAVEN, HALLOWED BE YOUR NAME, YOUR KINGDOM COME, YOUR WILL BE DONE, ON EARTH AS IT IS IN HEAVEN. GIVE US TODAY OUR DAILY BREAD. AND FORGIVE US OUR DEBTS, AS WE ALSO HAVE FORGIVEN OUR DEBTORS. AND LEAD US NOT INTO TEMPTATION, BUT DELIVER US FROM THE EVIL ONE.'"

MATTHEW 6:9-13

What is prayer, exactly?

Prayer is simply conversation with God. Don't worry if you don't hear His voice in an audible way. He has His own way of whispering to you and you may see it in Scripture as you prayerfully read God's Word.

Prayer is nothing more than taking time to talk to God. If you love Jesus, you will want to talk to Him. How should that conversation go you may ask? Don't over think it! If you were to talk to a trusted friend it would come naturally, wouldn't it? Think of prayer as if you talking to your most trusted friend. You can talk about the things that make you happy. You can share your fears and anxieties. The key is to be honest because nothing is hidden from Him. And nothing is out of bounds. That means you can literally say anything or ask anything and it will not shock Him. Even if you ask for things outside His will, it will not offend Him. He is the most trusted friend you will ever have. If you will be honest with Him, He will help you, guide you, and transform you. He will even change your desires so that they begin to align with His. Most importantly, you will grow more aware of His presence. You will grow closer to the God who made you.

Maybe you have trouble processing your thoughts or communicating. Try writing your prayers to God as if it's a text message or a letter. This can be part of your journaling experience. Journal your prayers to God and then record how He answers, even if it is months or years later. Remember, God always answers our prayers, it's just that sometimes His answer is no or wait. How did God answer your prayer? Record the answer. Later when you return to that journal and see God's faithfulness on display, your faith will be strengthened.

Don't spend a lot of time worrying about how to pray. God wants to hear from you. There is no use in using big churchy words to try and impress God. He knows your heart.

Using the Lord's Prayer as a guide (Matt. 6:9-13), write a short prayer to God, thanking Him, praising Him, confessing sin to Him, and asking for more of Him.

PRAY AT ALL TIMES IN THE SPIRIT WITH EVERY PRAYER AND REQUEST, AND STAY
ALERT WITH ALL PERSEVERANCE AND INTERCESSION FOR ALL THE SAINTS.

EPHESIANS 6:18

When should we pray? We are in a war. There is a battle going on right now in the spiritual realm that you may not see.

READ EPHESIANS 6:12-18.

We are in a battle and we need to be prayerful. There is a constant war going on around us that we cannot see. This should get our attention. Satan and the demons are plotting right now to trap and ruin you. The devil hates you and hates any child of God—he spends his time organizing ways to deceive and stop you. The enemy is most definitely at work and he has placed a target on your back. The life we are living is not to be taken lightly. It's serious business. Many people are tricked and trapped by sin. Lives are being destroyed. Let's fight against the enemy!

READ 1 PETER 5:8.

BE SOBER-MINDED, BE ALERT. YOUR ADVERSARY THE DEVIL IS PROWLING
AROUND LIKE A ROARING LION, LOOKING FOR ANYONE HE CAN DEVOUR.

READ EPHESIANS 6:18 AGAIN.

Notice how we should be in constant prayer. The author stresses the fact that we should be praying at all times. Then he continues with reminding us to stay alert.

Why should we stay alert in constant prayer?

Because of what Paul described in the first part of the passage. Life is a war and we are in it. Stay alert in constant prayer.

Do we have a good reason to pray? Is there danger out there?

How have you seen other lives devoured? How can you prevent it?

Find a quiet place to spend time in prayer. Remember to confess your sins, give thanks to God, and bring your requests before Him.

3 DEVOTION
STUDY DAY THREE

FOR I WILL POUR WATER ON THE THIRSTY LAND AND STREAMS
ON THE DRY GROUND; I WILL POUR OUT MY SPIRIT ON YOUR
DESCENDANTS AND MY BLESSING ON YOUR OFFSPRING.

ISAIAH 44:3

Why pray? Because God wants to bless you.

Why does He want to bless you? Because we, Christ followers, are His children. And the father loves His children. He blesses those He loves. He wants to bless His children and show His love This makes me happy. There is no question that the Father loves me. I have seen His love in so many ways. But sometimes my flesh lies to me and tricks me into thinking that God cannot be trusted as my good and perfect Father. My flesh wants me to believe that I have to earn love and acceptance from the Father. My flesh is very tricky and cannot be trusted. When we choose to pray, we are opening up the door for God to show us and remind us over and over that He wants to bless us and is worthy of our trust. He will watch over us.

What does He want to bless you with?

He wants to bless you, first, with His presence. You are His child and the good Father wants to bless His children.

God will pour out His Spirit and His blessings on you if you honestly and humbly seek Him. He will give water to thirsty land. When you are dry and thirsty and in need, He is there to bless you. He will do so because if you have trusted in Him, you are His child and He is a good Father.

Pray. He will bless you.

Read Job 22:26-27 and Isaiah 65:24.

How do we know God hears us?

What struggles or difficulties do you need to cry out to God for help in? Don't wait, cry out to Him now.

He always answers—sometimes it's *yes*, sometimes *no*, sometimes wait, and sometimes He says repent first and then we will talk.

"ASK, AND IT WILL BE GIVEN TO YOU. SEEK, AND YOU WILL FIND. KNOCK, AND THE DOOR WILL BE OPENED TO YOU. FOR EVERYONE WHO ASKS RECEIVES, AND THE ONE WHO SEEKS FINDS, AND TO THE ONE WHO KNOCKS, THE DOOR WILL BE OPENED. WHO AMONG YOU, IF HIS SON ASKS HIM FOR BREAD, WILL GIVE HIM A STONE? OR IF HE ASKS FOR A FISH, WILL GIVE HIM A SNAKE? IF YOU THEN, WHO ARE EVIL, KNOW HOW TO GIVE GOOD GIFTS TO YOUR CHILDREN, HOW MUCH MORE WILL YOUR FATHER IN HEAVEN GIVE GOOD THINGS TO THOSE WHO ASK HIM.

MATTHEW 7:7-11

Pray! Just pray.

We discussed earlier that we should pray because He is good and because He loves us. He also wants us to depend on Him and to come to Him. He wants our attention. He didn't have to promise us anything, but He did.

Jesus' intent in Matthew 7:7-11 is for us to ask. Ask and keep on asking. To knock and keep knocking. To seek and keep seeking. The emphasis is on our persistence. If we ask, knock, and seek, then He will give, bless, respond, rescue, reveal, and so on.

Remember prayer is not a magic wand that you just wave around and make things appear. It's not a trick you can use to get whatever you want. Prayer is the promise that God will take action when His children pray according to His will. We should not just pray for what we want, but for God to change our hearts and align them with His so we can honor Him.

So, have confidence that God listens when you talk to Him. Matthew 21:22 says "And if you believe, you will receive whatever you ask in prayer." Believe and pray in faith and watch what God does.

He is the good Father who wants to give good gifts to His children. Believe He is good.

Are you persistent in prayer? Why can this be difficult sometimes?

What are a few things from Scripture and this session that you need to dwell on and remember about prayer this week?

REJOICE ALWAYS, PRAY CONSTANTLY, GIVE THANKS IN EVERYTHING;
FOR THIS IS GOD'S WILL FOR YOU IN CHRIST JESUS. DON'T STIFLE
THE SPIRIT. DON'T DESPISE PROPHECIES, BUT TEST ALL THINGS. HOLD
ON TO WHAT IS GOOD. STAY AWAY FROM EVERY KIND OF EVIL.

1 THESSALONIANS 5:16-22

How should you pray?

We discussed earlier that we should always pray because there is a war against us in the spiritual realm. But you may ask, how should I pray? First, pray all the time, every chance you get. You don't have to bow your head and close your eyes. You can pray while riding in the car or walking or while you are in class after you have finished all your work. These can be short prayers that continually roll out of your mind. I strive to have an attitude of prayer. I like to be thanking God as I see things throughout my day. I like to thank Him for all of His blessings. I thank Him for His protection. I rejoice over all of the good things He has done for me. I love to thank Him for His death on the cross and resurrection. It's easy to be in prayer when we are thinking about how great God is.

I try and pray continually by asking God for small things as well as big things. I will pray for people I see in the community even if I don't know them. I will pray for pastors and missionaries. I will pray for anyone who crosses my mind during the day. These prayers oftentimes are not more than a few words. I am trying to align my heart with His so that I can be more like Jesus. This is what Christ following is about. Being a Christian is becoming more like Jesus. I have a long way to go. But the more I pray, the more I understand how to live like Jesus, think like Jesus, and love like Jesus.

Rejoice, give thanks in all circumstances. This is a great way to "set your minds on things above, not on earthly things" as it says in Colossians 3:2.

This will feed your spirit and starve the flesh.

> *What is God's will? Read 1 Thessalonians 5:18. It tells us exactly what God's will is—to pray and to rejoice.*

How are you praying? How are you rejoicing in the Lord?

HE ALSO TOLD THIS PARABLE TO SOME WHO TRUSTED IN THEMSELVES THAT THEY WERE RIGHTEOUS AND LOOKED DOWN ON EVERYONE ELSE: "TWO MEN WENT UP TO THE TEMPLE TO PRAY, ONE A PHARISEE AND THE OTHER A TAX COLLECTOR. THE PHARISEE WAS STANDING AND PRAYING LIKE THIS ABOUT HIMSELF: 'GOD, I THANK YOU THAT I'M NOT LIKE OTHER PEOPLE— GREEDY, UNRIGHTEOUS, ADULTERERS, OR EVEN LIKE THIS TAX COLLECTOR. I FAST TWICE A WEEK; I GIVE A TENTH OF EVERYTHING I GET.' "BUT THE TAX COLLECTOR, STANDING FAR OFF, WOULD NOT EVEN RAISE HIS EYES TO HEAVEN BUT KEPT STRIKING HIS CHEST AND SAYING, 'GOD, HAVE MERCY ON ME, A SINNER!' I TELL YOU, THIS ONE WENT DOWN TO HIS HOUSE JUSTIFIED RATHER THAN THE OTHER; BECAUSE EVERYONE WHO EXALTS HIMSELF WILL BE HUMBLED, BUT THE ONE WHO HUMBLES HIMSELF WILL BE EXALTED."

LUKE 18:9-14

Compare and contrast the prayers of the Pharisee and the tax collector in this parable. Whose prayer was honoring to God? Why?

What is humility? Why is it crucial to pray with humility? How might our pride hinder our prayers?

Have you ever heard someone else pray and thought to yourself, "I can't pray like that! I wouldn't even know where to start!" While Jesus is concerned with correcting those who trusted in themselves, the above parable tells us something about the type of prayer that honors God. He isn't impressed by those who know all the right things to say, nor is He moved to action when we pray the correct words. God wants us to be humble and honest when we pray. We must realize we are needy, but He is sufficient and He is our provider.

Don't worry about trying to figure out the right things to say to God. Rather, just be honest and ask God for help. When you cry out to God for help, you are admitting that He is greater and you need Him. Additionally, notice that the tax collector was honest about his sin. Perhaps lately you've felt like you don't measure up or you're not good enough to pray to God. If that's you, just admit this and ask for His forgiveness and mercy. The good news is that when we humbly ask for mercy, God gives it. We serve a God who loves to forgive His people when they cry out to Him. Remember the ultimate goal of prayer is to seek God.

SESSION 5

SOLITUDE

VIDEO — GUIDE

Begin by watching the video for Session 5. It starts with a few illusions that took Brock years of practice to perfect. The spiritual disciplines also take time to develop in our lives. We must practice them and make them a part of our daily lives.

BROCK INTRODUCES THE STUDY AND SHARES HOW WHEN ORANGE JUICE SETTLES, IT BECOMES MORE CLEAR. Similarly, when we get still, we can more clearly hear the whispers of God.

Living for Jesus doesn't happen overnight. We need to take time to get alone with God. Brock shares how this might mean saying no to some things. In our busy day-to-day lives, we need to prioritize solitude.

Where and when do you find the best time of solitude in your life?

How might you get away from others, get still, and listen to God this week?

On a scale of 1 to 10 (10 being the easiest and 1 being the most difficult), how would you rank the ease or difficulty for you to be still and quiet before God?

Why is it important for us to listen to God? How can we make this a greater priority in our lives?

Solitude feeds your spirit. Seek to schedule a time for reflection on God's Word and simply sit still and listen to God this week.

GROUP
DISCUSSION

I REMEMBER WHEN I GOT MY DRIVER'S LICENSE. I WAS GIVEN MY PARENTS' OLD CAR AND DECIDED TO DRIVE IT BY MYSELF FOR THE FIRST TIME. It was an old 1978 Pontiac; blueish in color, mixed with rust. The car was as long as a whale and weighed in at just under 30,000 pounds, I think. It would go from zero to sixty, eventually. It had an old radio with a dial tuner. We lived in the country and didn't have a clear radio station, so I had to patiently tune the radio just so until the signal would come through.

Living in the country, we did not have cable TV or internet. Our TV had these two metal antennas we called rabbit ears coming off the top. To get any TV shows to come through clearly, we had to point the rabbit ears in exactly the right direction. We even put foil on the end of the antennas to try and amplify the signal. The signal always seemed to be weak no matter what we did. But, if we were patient and positioned the antennas just right, we could get a signal and were able to sit down and clearly see a TV show.

Do you want to hear God's voice? You can hear it. It requires tuning your ears to hear His voice. You must train your spiritual ears to hear Him.

> *How can we hear God's voice? How can we tune our spiritual ears to listen to God's voice in our lives?*

Solitude. You must carve out time to be alone and still before God. You must prioritize the discipline of sitting at the feet of Jesus and tuning your heart to listen. He spoke the universe into existence. His voice is powerful but He often whispers. He speaks powerfully through His Word, but we must learn how to listen to even His whisper like Elijah did in 1 Kings 19. Solitude helps clear out the clutter that often keeps us from hearing His voice.

When I was 20, I realized I needed to learn how to hear God's voice. I have always heard of people saying that God spoke to them but I wanted to experience that for myself. I wanted that to be my lifestyle. So, I began getting up very early, before daylight. This was the most difficult thing for me to do because I am not a morning person. On top of that, I had to be at work at 7 am, so I would go to a park and meet with God. I will never forget the first time I experienced His presence. I remember reading Scripture and soon noticed God getting my attention through His Word and through nature. I learned to value that silence and solitude. And I began to learn how to meditate on Scripture.

> *How would you define solitude?*

> *Does deliberately getting alone to be with God come naturally to you? Why or why not?*

Solitude is purposefully spending time alone in silence. It's not being lonely, but it's getting alone for the purpose of meeting with God.

You can make this happen anywhere you can be alone. It could be in your room or backyard. In fact, getting out in nature can be helpful as it pulls us away from many of the things that so easily distract us. I have found that I can be "alone in solitude" anywhere, even on an airplane. Here is how. Get some headphones and put them in your ears. Even if you don't have any music to play, you can quickly find yourself tuning out everything around you and tuning in to listen to God.

Solitude will feed your spirit and starve your flesh. As you intentionally seek God in solitude, you are withdrawing from the world and walking into the presence of Jesus.

Jesus exemplified solitude many times throughout Scripture.

> **Read Mark 1:35 and discuss why Jesus was devoted to solitude.**
>
> *And rising very early in the morning, while it was still dark, he departed and went out to a desolate place, and there he prayed.*

Notice that he found a desolate place.

READ LUKE 5:16.

> **How might solitude boost your prayer life?**

Notice the word *often*. He did this often.

> *. . . those days He went out to the mountain to pray, and all night He continued in prayer to God. –Luke 6:12*

He prayed all night. Jesus prioritized solitude. If Jesus would get away early and often to pray, how much more do we need to make time to practice this discipline?

> **How often should we get alone with God?**

Here is a simple way to look at it. Once a day, once a week, once a month, and once a year.

Try to designate a brief time once a day to find solitude so you can pray, memorize Scripture, and worship. Set aside time each week to rest and allow God to fill you. Once a month, you could get away for a more devoted time of prayer and meditation on Scripture. Once a year, you could take a spiritual retreat. Okay, I realize that may sound far-fetched, but here is a possible way you could implement some of this. Maybe for a set time you could unplug. Put down the phone and stay away from computers and television for a day. Or maybe a week once a year. Use that time to free up space to allow God to move in closer. I have a feeling that you will love it.

BENEFITS OF SOLITUDE

Here are some great minds who had figured out the benefits of solitude. But more important than innovation or creativity, solitude opens space for God to speak. Solitude is when you stop shaking the orange juice bottle and let things settle so you can see clearly. See what? God's direction, His answers, or maybe just His presence. What a gift! Albert Einstein was a pretty smart dude. As a matter of fact, he is considered the father of modern physics (and he had cool hair).

Einstein understood solitude. He wrote: "On the other hand, although I have a regular work schedule, I take time to go for long walks on the beach so that I can listen to what is going on inside my head. If my work isn't going well, I lie down in the middle of a workday and gaze at the ceiling while I listen and visualize what goes on in my imagination."[1]

Nikola Tesla, the most innovative person in terms of electricity and our modern abilities to develop technology said, "The mind is sharper and keener in seclusion and uninterrupted solitude. Originality thrives in seclusion free of outside influences beating upon us to cripple the creative mind. Be alone, that is the secret of invention; be alone, that is when ideas are born."[2]

Picasso said "Without great solitude no serious work is possible."[3]

Perhaps some people do not have solitude because of fear? Maybe they are fearful that they will get bored or scared or miss out on something. Perhaps we are scared of slowing down for fear of not being able to get things done. Maybe we are all too busy.

MAKING TIME FOR SOLITUDE

What does solitude look like? What might it look like for you to engage in this discipline?

Productive solitude is not an exact science. But here is an idea. Start by finding the time. Even if you must give up something. Most people have the time but they fail to intentionally make solitude a priority. Spend time in prayer—listening to Him and pouring your thoughts out to God. Read Scripture, worship, or spend some time journaling or meditating on Scripture. Most of all, just allow your mind to settle and expect to experience God's nearness. With some practice you will begin to experience God in a way that will be exhilarating.

The purpose of solitude is not to fill yourself up so that you are more self-sufficient, but to grow to be more reliant on God. Jesus was fully God and fully man—He willingly embraced the weaknesses and limitations that come from being human. As a man, Jesus disciplined Himself to be alone as a means of leaning fully on God and submitting fully to His will.

Some people choose to write their prayers in a journal. Meditation is simply contemplation—thinking about God and His truths as He reveals promises and His character. Meditate on His Word and apply it to your life.

You can't cram solitude. You must plan.

> Set your minds on things above, not on earthly things. —Colossians 3:2

To starve the flesh and feed your spirit, you must set your minds on Christ and those things which honor Him. What things? Read Philippians 4:8-9.

> Finally brothers and sisters, whatever is true, whatever is honorable, whatever is just, whatever is pure, whatever is lovely, whatever is commendable—if there is any moral excellence and if there is anything praiseworthy—dwell on these things. Do what you have learned and received and heard from me, and seen in me, and the God of peace will be with you.

What are some things that rob you from solitude? How might you make solitude a priority this week?

Your relationship with your digital devices, constant communication, Netflix, fear of boredom, social media, anything that consumes our mental energy such that we can't slow down—each of these have the potential to rob us of tapping into the benefits of solitude. However, it's not merely outward things

The purpose of solitude is not to fill yourself up so that you are more self-sufficient, but to grow to be more reliant on God.

that can keep us from tapping into the benefits of solitude, it's also our inner attitudes—our compulsion to compare ourselves to others, or our drive for success.

You need a rhythm—like music. A song has a verse and a chorus and then breaks between each of them for the singer to inhale.

Think about our need for oxygen and how you can't stay underwater long before you will need to breathe. Solitude is like oxygen for our souls.

> Stop your fighting, and know that I am God, exalted among the nations, exalted on the earth. —Psalm 46:10

The ESV and several other translations say "Be still," while the CSB says "Stop your fighting." Either translation reminds us to make time for solitude and to dwell on the character of God and who He is. He is exalted not only among the nations, but also on the earth. Give Him the glory that is due to Him this week and spend time in solitude listening to Him.

1

DEVOTION
STUDY DAY ONE

BUT WHEN YOU PRAY, GO INTO YOUR PRIVATE ROOM, SHUT YOUR
DOOR, AND PRAY TO YOUR FATHER WHO IS IN SECRET. AND
YOUR FATHER WHO SEES IN SECRET WILL REWARD YOU.

MATTHEW 6:6

If you want to grow closer to God, you need to spend some time in solitude. When we get alone and get still, we can grow in intimacy with the God who made us.

READ MATTHEW 6:6 AGAIN.

Why is it important that you make time to spend alone with God?

Have you ever heard the saying, "Love is spelled T-I-M-E"? If you love someone, you will want to spend quality time with him or her. The more time you spend together, the more it will begin to bother you when you are away. To be separated from someone you love creates a longing that compels you to find a way to spend time with them.

It's very difficult to love someone when you choose not to spend time with them. This is why FaceTime and Skype were created. We have some family who are missionaries in Peru. They spend a few years at a time in the Amazon jungle working with the local people there. All three of their children were born there in Peru. We will often all gather around a computer screen and make a Skype or FaceTime call. It's not the same as being in the same room but it was the best we could do. My point is, we made an effort to see them every chance we could.

Solitude is about quality time with God the Father. He wants us to give Him our undivided attention.

Have you ever been interrupted or distracted when trying to have a conversation with someone? Maybe someone kept calling or texting, or maybe you did not realize the pressing nature of the issue or situation at the time and simply felt bothered. Can you imagine that scenario and feel the frustration on the other end of the one trying to communicate with you? I think God may feel the same way when we are distracted and not spending time with Him. Solitude is simply eliminating distractions so you can talk to Jesus and hear from Him. Listening is key. When the distractions are gone, the intimacy of God is near. That's quality time. That's solitude.

How will you eliminate distractions this week so you can focus on listening to God?

DEVOTION
STUDY DAY TWO 2 ————

BECAUSE IF ANYONE IS A HEARER OF THE WORD AND NOT A DOER, HE IS LIKE
SOMEONE LOOKING AT HIS OWN FACE IN A MIRROR. FOR HE LOOKS AT HIMSELF,
GOES AWAY, AND IMMEDIATELY FORGETS WHAT KIND OF PERSON HE WAS.

JAMES 1:23-24

Meditation. The word *meditation* is a confusing term. Some people hear meditation and think of Eastern religious practices, or transcendental meditation where people think they can fly. These sorts of things are not at all what the Bible has in mind when it refers to meditation.

One day, we went to the beach. When we arrived, we noticed a guy meditating by sitting with his legs crossed on a beach towel. He would begin to shake and convulse as if he were out of control. He shook violently until his phone rang, then he would check his phone and then go right back to shaking around. It was wild to watch. This is not the type of meditation I am talking about. The type of meditation the Bible calls us to practice is completely different.

Biblical meditation is not letting go of our minds and ourselves, but rather focusing our minds on truth. Christian meditation requires contemplation—deliberately focusing on the truth of God's Word. We need to prepare our minds to deeply consider the truths and promises of God in Scripture, looking for meaning and application to our lives.

> *Read James 1:23-24 again. How does James describe those who hear God's Word but fail to put it into action?*

Meditation gives us a chance to think about the truths of God and to apply those truths. Thinking on these truths that we read in the Word is such a great way to find God's will. He will guide us and we will have the right direction in life when we meditate on His Word daily.

READ PHILIPPIANS 4:8.

It says to think on these things—these things will feed your spirit.

> *Why is it important that you worship God with both your heart and your mind?*

> *What, specifically, could you think on this week as a means of seeking God and growing in your relationship with Him?*

JESUS CAME NEAR AND SAID TO THEM, "ALL AUTHORITY HAS BEEN GIVEN TO ME IN HEAVEN AND ON EARTH. GO, THEREFORE, AND MAKE DISCIPLES OF ALL NATIONS, BAPTIZING THEM IN THE NAME OF THE FATHER AND OF THE SON AND OF THE HOLY SPIRIT, TEACHING THEM TO OBSERVE EVERYTHING I HAVE COMMANDED YOU. AND REMEMBER, I AM WITH YOU ALWAYS, TO THE END OF THE AGE."

MATTHEW 28:18-20

The passenger.

When I was 22 years old I had to drive an hour to get to work. I didn't have a radio or any other digital device at the time. I would get into my truck and clear a spot on the passenger seat as if someone was riding with me. I would save that seat for Jesus to ride with me.

I know what you are thinking, this is super cheesy! I know I didn't need to leave this seat open for Jesus to be with me. I know that God is with me at all times, but it helped me actively think about Christ so that I might pray more freely as I actively acknowledged His presence with me there in the truck.

> *What was the last thing Jesus said to His disciples in the Great Commission (v. 20)? Why do you think they needed this reminder?*

Clearing off the seat next to you in your car or at the table might not help you or it might be too cheesy for you. However, here is what I know, you need to constantly remind yourself of God's presence in your life. One of the last things Jesus said to His disciples was that He would always be with them (Matt. 28:20).

We need to actually believe that Jesus is with us. We need to realize that we are never truly alone—as Christ followers, our Savior is with us at all times.

> *How might you more actively acknowledge Christ's presence in your daily life?*

Solitude is about creating space for God. Creating a place for you and Him to meet and spend quality time.

> *How can you create space in your life to be alone with God?*

NOW MOSES TOOK A TENT AND PITCHED IT OUTSIDE THE CAMP, AT A DISTANCE
FROM THE CAMP; HE CALLED IT THE TENT OF MEETING. ANYONE WHO WANTED
TO CONSULT THE LORD WOULD GO TO THE TENT OF MEETING THAT WAS
OUTSIDE THE CAMP. WHENEVER MOSES WENT OUT TO THE TENT, ALL THE
PEOPLE WOULD STAND UP, EACH ONE AT THE DOOR OF HIS TENT, AND THEY
WOULD WATCH MOSES UNTIL HE ENTERED THE TENT. WHEN MOSES ENTERED
THE TENT, THE PILLAR OF CLOUD WOULD COME DOWN AND REMAIN AT THE
ENTRANCE TO THE TENT, AND THE LORD WOULD SPEAK WITH MOSES.

EXODUS 33:7-9

Moses created space for solitude. He followed God's lead in building the tent of meeting which allowed him to be alone with God.

You can see that when Moses purposefully had solitude with the Lord, God came and spoke "face to face." Amazing! I wonder what is was like to meet face to face with God. To hear God's voice face-to-face seems so incredible! You may not see God face-to-face but, in faith, you can know that He is near, He is listening and He is ready.

I want to meet with God and hear Him talk to me like He did with Moses. I want to hear from God like a friend. I can't imagine how incredible it was for Moses to just hang out with God like a friend. I long for the day that I can sit face-to-face and have a conversation with God and actually see Him. But until then I will be satisfied with making time to be alone with Him here. His presence still brings joy even if it doesn't come with a cloud over the entrance of our door.

How would it feel to talk to God face-to-face?

How can you create space for solitude?

What is one step you will take this week to make space for time alone with God in prayer and in His Word?

THEN HE SAID, "GO OUT AND STAND ON THE MOUNTAIN IN THE LORD'S PRESENCE." AT THAT MOMENT, THE LORD PASSED BY. A GREAT AND MIGHTY WIND WAS TEARING AT THE MOUNTAINS AND WAS SHATTERING CLIFFS BEFORE THE LORD, BUT THE LORD WAS NOT IN THE WIND. AFTER THE WIND THERE WAS AN EARTHQUAKE, BUT THE LORD WAS NOT IN THE EARTHQUAKE. AFTER THE EARTHQUAKE THERE WAS A FIRE, BUT THE LORD WAS NOT IN THE FIRE. AND AFTER THE FIRE THERE WAS A VOICE, A SOFT WHISPER. WHEN ELIJAH HEARD IT, HE WRAPPED HIS FACE IN HIS MANTLE AND WENT OUT AND STOOD AT THE ENTRANCE OF THE CAVE.

1 KINGS 19:11-13

Here is the backdrop for this story. Elijah was on the run, hiding from those who were trying to kill him. The Lord led Elijah into a mountain cave where he spent the night and the most incredible thing happened! There was an earthquake, a tornado, a fire, and then a small whisper.

I love this. God spoke to Elijah with a whisper. There was the power of a tornado, earthquake, and even a fire, but God chose to speak in the form of a whisper. The contrast was obvious. Imagine the loud roar of a tornado. Imagine the rumble of an earthquake. Think about the blazing sound of a big fire. Compare these to a soft whisper.

God is whispering to us every time we read His Word. If God whispers, we must get still to hear it. That's why solitude is so important. Uninterrupted solitude is one of the best ways to hear from God. Solitude minimizes distractions, clears our minds, and helps us focus on seeking God in prayer and Bible study.

God whispered to Elijah and gave him direction. God met with Elijah in solitude. It was a powerful moment.

How can you make sure you hear the whispers of God?

How has God been whispering to you lately? How will you respond?

ON THE SEVENTH DAY GOD HAD COMPLETED HIS WORK THAT HE HAD
DONE, AND HE RESTED ON THE SEVENTH DAY FROM ALL HIS WORK
THAT HE HAD DONE. GOD BLESSED THE SEVENTH DAY AND DECLARED
IT HOLY, FOR ON IT HE RESTED FROM ALL HIS WORK OF CREATION.

GENESIS 2:2-3

Every Tuesday, I do something a little out of the ordinary. I make it my Sabbath. Let me explain.

I am traveling almost every week to do ministry in some part of the world. Almost every weekend, including Sunday, I am working at a church. Most times I am traveling back home on Monday. Therefore Tuesday is generally the day I find myself needing a break from work. Truthfully, there is never a natural time for me to rest. I always have work to do. I always have someone needing me to answer a call or an email. The same is probably true for you. However, I force myself to rest because I know it's good for me. To make time to rest, however, I have to have a plan. My plan looks something like this.

I take time off and devote it to three things. The morning is for me and God to hang out. I use this time to read Scripture and other devotional books. Then I just allow time to be still and meditate and listen for the whispers of God. I make sure that my phone is turned off and I stay away from computers. I will oftentimes find a coffee shop or a place in nature to get this day of solitude and rest kicked off. The afternoon is for time by myself doing something I enjoy, like a hobby. In the evening, I have a date night with my wife. I have learned that I need to invest in this relationship in the same way I invest in my spiritual life. I have found these days to be tremendously rejuvenating. The flesh will try and tell me that I can't afford to take a day off. The truth is, spiritually speaking, I can't afford not to take a day off.

I have to plan for solitude, otherwise my tendency to overwork myself will take over. I must find a day that I can set aside to rest and focus on God. The point of the Sabbath is not the day of the week, but that we set aside time to rest, worship, and focus on God. Solitude feeds the Spirit.

READ JOHN 15:1-11.

What time can you designate to have a restful Sabbath?

What might your Sabbath routine look like? How could you start this week?

SESSION 6

FASTING

VIDEO

GUIDE

Start by watching the video for Session 6. It opens with a stunt with a bow, an arrow, and a bell. Brock explains how the stunt requires laser-beam focus. Likewise, our walks with the Lord require intense focus. Brock shares how fasting helps him focus on Jesus. The purpose of fasting is to focus on God and it requires a plan.

JESUS BEGAN HIS MINISTRY BY FASTING WHICH HELPED HIM MAINTAIN LASER-BEAM FOCUS. JESUS ILLUSTRATED HOW WE CAN FOCUS ON CHRIST THROUGH FASTING.

> *What do you know about fasting? Have you ever fasted before?*
>
> *Why is it important for us to focus? What things in your life most often distract you from following and seeking Christ?*
>
> *Why are the motives for our fasting important?*
>
> *Is fasting supposed to be a private or public spiritual discipline (see Matt. 6:18)? Why do you think that is?*
>
> *If you have never fasted before, pray about doing so and consider if God might be leading you to fast for a period of time. Be sure to consult your leaders and a doctor before doing so.*

Take some time to reflect on the spiritual disciplines that we've studied so far. What is God teaching you through this study? The spiritual disciplines should help us to feed the spirit rather than the flesh. Pray that God would help you grow in your walk with Him and in the seven spiritual disciplines we're studying over the course of this Bible study.

FASTING. WHAT IS IT?

Well, to be honest, fasting is simply taking a short, deliberate break from eating.

The biblical references to fasting refer to taking such breaks from food and, in some rare cases, from food and drink.

> *Even now—this is the LORD's declaration—turn to me with all your heart, with fasting, weeping, and mourning. —Joel 2:12*

> ***How might abstaining from food for a time help you to give more of your heart to the Lord?***

Other religions also define fasting as giving up food. Lately there has been a trend to redefine fasting as anything someone might give up for a time, like many people do for Lent. For example, some people will fast from listening to country music. Well, that's great if you want to give up the twang for a few days, but there is much more to fasting from a biblical perspective.

We sometimes look for an easier way to satisfy the discipline of fasting by redefining it to suit our desires. We will redefine fasting to be whatever we want, such as fasting from video games, watching sports, and so on. There is definite value in abstaining from things for a time to break habits or to free up time. Remember, however, the practice of fasting as mentioned in Scripture refers to abstaining from food.

- Jesus fasted 40 days in the desert before He began His ministry (Matt. 4:1-11).
- Moses fasted 40 days when he met with God and received the Ten Commandments (Ex. 34:20).
- Daniel fasted 21 days when he was in Babylon (Dan. 10:1-2).
- The disciples often fasted prior to making important decisions in which they needed God's guidance (Acts 13:3; 14:23).

Throughout the Old Testament, you will find people or communities who fasted while in mourning or when they were desperate and needed to be reminded of God's presence.

Fasting is biblical. Fasting is normal. Fasting is not just for weirdos. Fasting is for us.

You may hear people say that it's dangerous to fast. However, when done right, fasting is healthy. Mark Mattson, professor or neuroscience at Johns Hopkins School of Medicine claims that fasting actually "bolsters brain activity."[1] There are neurochemical changes in the brain when you fast. Fasting is good for the body.

According to Mattson, "Fasting enhances the ability of neurons to cope with stress and resist diseases. It stimulates antioxidant defenses, promotes clearance of molecular 'garbage,' enhances DNA repair, and reduces inflammation." [2]

Don't accept the notion that fasting is unhealthy. People are uneasy about fasting because it is neither talked about nor celebrated very often in the modern Christian church. I personally would like to see that change.

You should never fast to lose weight or get a "better body." Fasting won't do that for you. Fasting to lose weight is dangerous. Fasting should never be entered into lightly, particularly if you have ever suffered from an eating disorder. If you fast to look better physically or even to appear more holy to the people around you, you've missed the point.

So, what's the purpose of fasting? How might fasting help us to feed our spirit?

The purpose of fasting is dependence on God. You need more of God in your life. You want more of Him in your life. You are desperate for God to act or reveal or move. Fasting is about passionately seeking God. Fasting is the act of drawing closer to God and saying you would rather have Him than food. When you fast, you are becoming and acting desperate for God to be more real in your life, relationships, city, or culture.

When you fast, you get very serious about your prayer life. During times of fasting, you will grow closer to God and your prayers will become more desperate and focused. You will stop throwing up last minute prayers to God before you fall asleep or before you hop on the computer.

While fasting, prayer is never an afterthought. Instead, prayer becomes the focal point. Each time you feel hungry you are reminded to pray. And when you are hungry for hours at a time or days at a time, you make sure those prayers are serious.

WHAT SHOULD I EXPECT WHEN I FAST?

Expect to get hungry. That may sound funny because it's so obvious. Your flesh will respond and try to argue with your decision to stay away from food. You may not feel thirsty, but you will be. You will get dehydrated quickly if you do not drink more than usual. You may get a weird taste in your mouth. Don't worry, that's normal. Your brain may be more alert. For some, you may feel like you have more energy at times, while others may feel fatigue more quickly.

Fasting exposes our idols and shows us how much we rely on ourselves. The flesh begins to churn and things begin to bubble up during a fast. The flesh awakens and wants to argue. The flesh wants to convince you that it is in control. The flesh will get restless as you starve it, but your spirit will come alive!

Fasting is a beautiful thing. Some of my most special memories are during my times of fasting. Some of the greatest times when I could hear God guide me or reveal Himself to me were through fasting.

If you fast with right motives, you will begin praying more desperately. When you fast, you will pray with determination and passion. When you fast, you will be relentless in prayer because you will feel your need for God. Your hunger will drive you to pray more often and more intently. When you fast, you are literally saying that you are hungrier for God than food.

Fasting does not make God love you more. If you are a believer, you already possess God's love because of the finished work of Jesus. You don't have to work your way into God's love through works and deeds. We fast not to earn God's love, but to delight more deeply in it—to grow in our desperation for Christ.

How often should you fast? How long should you fast? What is appropriate?

There is no good answer for that. The Bible doesn't mandate a certain time or place for you to fast. It is just expected. Since you are a teenager and your body is still rapidly growing, make sure you talk to an adult and your doctor before you practice this discipline.

There have been periods where I fasted one day per month. I've even had seasons where I felt compelled to fast one day per week. And there are some historic times in my faith where I was determined to fast for several days in a row.

When I was 22, I was working a blue-collar job at a sawmill in Arkansas. I was living in Texas and had to drive a good distance to get to work each night. At work, I wore ear plugs because of the loud noise, so I had very little time to talk to other people. Instead, I began to pray. I realized God was asking me to fast in order to draw closer to Him. As I fasted, I spent my time praying and seeking God. He clearly laid out His plans for my ministry during those sweet times of prayer and fasting.

> ### We fast not to earn God's love, but to delight more deeply in it—to grow in our desperation for Christ.

Later in life when I had been on the road doing ministry for many years, I was once again led by God to do a longer fast. This time it was 40 days. It seemed a little overwhelming to not eat for that long. I don't advise anyone to try this unless you are cleared by your doctor and have sought the counsel of Christian adults and mentors. This is just my story.

I entered that fast with enthusiasm thinking I'd get fresh, innovative ideas or insight that would take my ministry to the next level.

That didn't happen. I got something even greater. As I drew closer to Him, He made Himself more real. I heard His voice, and He began changing me. Rather than having some big revelation, God simply began revealing my sin and pride on day one. He revealed Himself to me in His Word—impressing key attributes of His character onto my heart and mind.

HERE IS AN EASY WAY TO FAST WITHOUT WORRYING ABOUT ANY HEALTH CONCERNS.

This worked well for me and I encourage others to try this: pick a day each month. My wife and I chose the first weekend of the month. Start on Saturday night when the sun goes down and do not eat (but drink plenty of water) until the sun goes down on Sunday. Essentially, you don't eat for 24 hours. Maybe a late lunch or an early dinner Saturday then start your intentional fast. Skip breakfast and lunch on Sunday and then eat dinner Sunday night to break your fast.

I think you will find that it is easier than you may have imagined. I think, at times, you will find it exciting and look forward to it. If you are not excited about it, then change it up and try something else.

What would happen if students across the nation had an ongoing lifestyle of fasting?

What would happen if we were all fasting and praying for our church leaders, pastors, and people at our churches? What would happen if people across the land were drawing close to God on a regular basis?

> [Christ] must increase, but I must decrease. —John 3:30

I believe we would see a different culture. We would see people being the salt and light that Scripture teaches. People who are being changed to become more like Jesus as passionate followers, living out our faith. We might just see a revival!

In *Habits of Grace: Enjoying Jesus through the Spiritual Disciplines*, John Piper is quoted: "Fasting is the physical exclamation point at the end of the sentence, 'This much, O God, I want you.'"[3]

WHEN SHOULD YOU FAST?

When mourning, when you need direction, when you need to make sure you hear His voice, when starting a new ministry, when you want to.

WHEN SHOULD YOU NOT FAST?

If your doctor says not to. If you have a medical condition that would make fasting harmful. If your purpose is to lose weight. If you plan to do a physical activity that requires a high calorie diet, i.e. running a marathon or playing a competitive sport.

It's difficult to fast when you are comfortable, or when you have everything you want and need. It's difficult to fast when you are content in your sin.

It's easy to fast when you are disturbed. It's easy to fast when you are passionate for God to move. It's easy to fast when you want God to reveal truth or when you are broken. It's easy to fast when you are under persecution or when you are oppressed.

Fasting gives you focus. Laser-beam focus.

TEAR YOUR HEARTS, NOT JUST YOUR CLOTHES, AND RETURN TO THE LORD YOUR GOD. FOR HE IS GRACIOUS AND COMPASSIONATE, SLOW TO ANGER, ABOUNDING IN FAITHFUL LOVE, AND HE RELENTS FROM SENDING DISASTER. WHO KNOWS? HE MAY TURN AND RELENT AND LEAVE A BLESSING BEHIND HIM, SO YOU CAN OFFER GRAIN AND WINE TO THE LORD YOUR GOD.

JOEL 2:13-14

How do we know that it's time to fast?

Simply put, fasting is about growing in your desperation for God.

There have been times in my life where I felt the nudge from the Holy Spirit to fast. Sometimes I was wanting to fast to seek His will for my life and ministry. There have been times when my priorities seemed to be out of focus, or maybe straight up rotten. I remember being so desperate to be with God that I needed to fast. Fasting is such a beautiful thing. I can think of no better way to reset our hearts and priorities.

Joel lived among people who had turned their backs on God. They were seeing an agricultural plague of locusts that motivated him to call the people to repent and fast to avoid the coming destruction and further damage. The answer as to when to repent is always now—don't put off turning away from sin and seeking God's face. When God nudges you to fast, then the time to obey is now. Let Him prepare your heart for a fast. Always fast carefully and with accountability. If you sense the Lord leading you to fast, share this with a Christian mentor or parent and start thinking and praying about what that might look like.

> *How might fasting help you focus on drawing near to Christ? How might it help you grow in your desperation for God?*

> *Have you ever discussed whether a short fast might be appropriate for you with a parent or adult Christian mentor? Make plans to do so this week?*

THE GREATEST AMONG YOU WILL BE YOUR SERVANT.
WHOEVER EXALTS HIMSELF WILL BE HUMBLED, AND
WHOEVER HUMBLES HIMSELF WILL BE EXALTED.

MATTHEW 23:11-12

What are the benefits of fasting? This may seem like the wrong question to ask, but let's explore this further.

The first benefit is obedience. Faithful obedience to God is always a blessing, it brings freedom. It frees the mind of guilt and lessens the power of temptation. Obeying God can have a momentous effect. When you are doing what's right, it's easier to continue doing what is right. When you are living in sin, it's easy to continue living in sin. During times of fasting you will notice your heart and brain begin aligning with God. Obedience will always naturally follow.

Another benefit I've experienced from fasting is power. In fasting, your prayer life gets better and with more prayer comes more power. What power? Power over sin, power in ministry, God's power experienced in your life. Why do we see God's power increase in our lives when we pray more often? Simple, when we truly pray, we are humbling ourselves and admitting our weaknesses. We must confess our need for His perfect strength.

Begin with fasting, and let your prayer life grow. During times of prayer and fasting you will see God increase in power over your life. You will see how real He truly is.

READ MATTHEW 23:11-12 AGAIN.

> *Notice that it says those who are humble will be exalted. Exalted by whom? God Almighty.*

READ JAMES 4:6.

> *Who does God oppose?*

Those who are proud. The most obvious symptom of pride is prayerlessness. If you do not pray, then you can be sure of one thing: you are a proud person. But God shows favor to the humble. How do we become humble? The best way I know is to start with prayer and fasting. To fast is to run to Jesus. To fast is to deny the flesh and its desires for the sake of knowing our Savior with greater affection and intimacy.

> *What are other benefits to fasting you can think of?*

WHENEVER YOU FAST, DON'T BE GLOOMY LIKE THE HYPOCRITES. FOR THEY MAKE THEIR FACES UNATTRACTIVE SO THAT THEIR FASTING IS OBVIOUS TO PEOPLE. TRULY I TELL YOU, THEY HAVE THEIR REWARD.

MATTHEW 6:16

Prayer and fasting. They go together. If you fast without praying, then you are not really fasting. That would be more like a hunger strike.

In 2003, the world famous magician David Blaine locked himself into a glass box over the River Thames in England for 44 days. It was a huge spectacle. Some people were not sure if it was real or an illusion. I saw it on TV and it sure looked real to me. What's interesting about this stunt is that he didn't eat for the entire 44 days. It was self-inflicted starvation that brought about much controversy and attention. It was very a bold stunt to promote his TV show on ABC (please don't ever try doing something like this, by the way). But, Blaine swore off food for a month and a half to promote himself. He lost a significant amount of body mass in the process and at the end of 44 days, he was taken straight to a hospital. The whole thing was quite strange because so many people were watching. It became worldwide news.

That's not a spiritual fast. Fasting really should be more private than this. Blaine had thousands of people watching him and each day he became a little more emaciated. When we fast, we must not make a public spectacle out of it (Matt. 6:16).

> *Read Matthew 6:16 again. What is the purpose of fasting? What must not be the purpose?*

> *How might you pray and fast and seek God for the right kind of reward?*

We need to fast in humility with the emphasis being on prayer. Anyone can fast, but it takes us being very careful to not use fasting as a way to get attention.

MY FLESH AND MY HEART MAY FAIL, BUT GOD IS THE STRENGTH
OF MY HEART, MY PORTION FOREVER. THOSE FAR FROM YOU WILL
CERTAINLY PERISH; YOU DESTROY ALL WHO ARE UNFAITHFUL TO
YOU. BUT AS FOR ME, GOD'S PRESENCE IS MY GOOD. I HAVE MADE
THE LORD GOD MY REFUGE, SO I CAN TELL ABOUT ALL YOU DO.

PSALM 73:26-28

The great hunger strike.

Many people have gone without food for a certain cause. Over the past few decades we have
seen people use a hunger strike as a method for getting their agenda across to the public or the
government. Nelson Mandela had a hunger strike in 1966 to protest prison conditions in South
Africa. Hunger strikes are not a new thing. Whether we agree with the cause or not, the truth
is hunger strikes get people's attention. Biblical fasting is not a hunger strike. Some people see
fasting as a way to get God's attention and compel Him to act on our behalf. God cannot be
manipulated into action. Fasting neither impresses God nor shocks Him into action.

God already knows what we need. Fasting is for us. It changes us and should make us more like
Jesus. It's not a way to force God to do something. If we are going to fast, we must remember it
is a chance for us to become more like Him. We draw near to Him and allow that to be the goal.
Sometimes people may be tempted to fast so that a circumstance will change. They may think
that if they fast, then God may change a bad circumstance and problems can be avoided. The
truth is that may or may not happen. God is in charge and can do as He sees fit. Our hope as we
fast should not be that God would change our lives or circumstances, but our hope should be for
God Himself—we should long to be closer to Him and more like Him.

Fasting is not a hunger strike to force God to give us attention. He is God, He already knows
what's going on. We need to draw close to Him and allow His presence to be the goal.

> *Read Psalm 73:23-28. How might you draw near to God this week?*

> *What should you expect from Him as you do so?*

BUT AS THE ONE WHO CALLED YOU IS HOLY, YOU ALSO ARE TO BE HOLY IN
ALL YOUR CONDUCT; FOR IT IS WRITTEN, BE HOLY, BECAUSE I AM HOLY.

1 PETER 1:15-16

Fasting helps us see our sin. Fasting gives us the opportunity to repent.

Fasting can help us slow down enough to focus on God's presence in our lives. In His presence we can see how holy He is—more holy than we can comprehend. In the presence of a holy God our sin becomes very evident. In those moments we have the opportunity to repent and experience freedom from sin.

How holy is God? In the Book of Revelation there are angels who constantly sing "holy, holy, holy." When a word is repeated in Greek three times in a row, it's like saying that it's the most extreme. So when we see "holy, holy, holy," it communicates that there is none more holy. He is the epitome of holiness to the extreme. What does holy actually mean? It literally means *without sin*, *set apart*, or *without blemish*. When something even slightly unholy comes near something holy, then the "slightly unholy" thing will quickly be seen as completely unholy. In Exodus 19:12, because of God's holiness, people are not even allowed to go near the mountain where God gave Moses the Law. If someone even touched the edge of the mountain, he or she would die. That's how serious His holiness is. He is beyond anything we can imagine, therefore repentance must be a central part of our fasting experience.

What is repentance?

How might fasting, when approached carefully and humbly, lead to repentance?

We don't usually hear the word *repentance* outside of church. What is it?

It means to change direction. It's a change of attitude. When our heart takes a 180 degree turn, that is repentance. However, repentance is not just a change of direction physically. We must also have a change of mind and heart. We must look to Christ to change our hearts so that we will begin moving and living in the direction He has for us.

We need to turn from sin. Fasting gives us a chance to see our sin and repent. When we fast out of a humble desire for Christ, it leads to godliness.

THEN JESUS LEFT THE JORDAN, FULL OF THE HOLY SPIRIT, AND WAS LED
BY THE SPIRIT IN THE WILDERNESS FOR FORTY DAYS TO BE TEMPTED
BY THE DEVIL. HE ATE NOTHING DURING THOSE DAYS, AND WHEN THEY
WERE OVER, HE WAS HUNGRY. THE DEVIL SAID TO HIM, "IF YOU ARE
THE SON OF GOD, TELL THIS STONE TO BECOME BREAD." BUT JESUS
ANSWERED HIM, "IT IS WRITTEN: MAN MUST NOT LIVE ON BREAD ALONE."

LUKE 4:1-4

READ LUKE 4:1-13.

Why do you think Jesus fasted prior to beginning His public ministry?

How might fasting help you to lean more heavily on God? How might it help you trust Him more?

Fasting is the beginning. It reminds us of how desperately we need God for everything. No one likes to be needy but in our relationship with God, neediness is a good thing. Our neediness honors God when we look to Him to fill us with what we are lacking. In other words, in admitting our neediness, we are acknowledging God's sufficiency. When we fast with the right motive—to draw near to God—He blesses us with more of Himself and launches us out into the world with a renewed sense of hope, strength, and purpose.

Jesus' fasting was a launchpad for His public ministry. It all began with fasting.

He went into the desert and met with God. He returned full of the power in the Spirit.

As Luke 4:4 references how we "must not live on bread alone," we are reminded of the importance of being fed spiritually. One of the best ways to launch a ministry is by fasting. The best way to continue ministry is fasting. Fasting is good for your walk with Christ and for your ministry. We are all called to ministry in our homes, schools, neighborhoods, and around the world (Matt. 28:18-20).

Talk to a parent or church leader about fasting as a means to grow in your walk with Christ so that you might live more fully on mission for Him. As a teenager, your body is growing and changing rapidly and involving an adult in your fast will help you make sure you fast in a manner that is safe and does not do harm to your body.

MINISTRY

Begin by watching the video for Session 7. It starts with an illusion with red balls. Brock shares how we are all called to do ministry. He defines ministry simply as showing love and speaking truth.

> *What do you think it means to minister to others?*

> *Where do you see yourself in ministry? What spiritual gifts might you be able to use as you serve?*

> *How have you served previously, and how is God calling you to minister to those around you today?*

PASTORS AREN'T THE ONLY ONES CALLED TO MINISTRY. YOUR MISSION FIELD IS RIGHT WHERE YOU ARE. GOD HAS CALLED YOU TO SHARE THE GOSPEL.

> *How are you being discipled? By whom?*

> *How are you discipling others? Is there someone you need to reach out to and share the love of Christ with this week?*

> *What other spiritual disciplines that we have studied do you need to carve out time to practice more?*

Ministry feeds your spirit. Pray that God will give you opportunities to minister to those who you come in contact with this week. Not only do you need to minister to others, but you also need to be ministered to by other believers, so seek to be a part of a local church body. Ministry begins in the local church and then bleeds out into the world around us. The church is not simply a building, but is the global body of believers serving day-to-day in the corner of the world where God has placed and called them to serve and minister.

GROUP
DISCUSSION

WHEN I WAS IN COLLEGE, A WISE MAN TOLD ME THAT IF I COULD FIND SOMETHING I LIKED TO DO, THEN I WOULD NEVER HAVE TO WORK A DAY IN MY LIFE. Some people love what they do and therefore it doesn't feel like work. I have some great news: ministry is the same way. When we find what we love to do in ministry, it rarely feels like a chore. Doing ministry, using the gifts and talents God has given you, brings great joy.

What comes to mind when you hear the word ministry?

I became a follower of Christ when I was 15. I fully surrendered my life to Jesus and immediately began looking for ways to serve Him. I wasn't sure how ministry worked or how I fit in because I wasn't a pastor, worship leader, or a missionary. But, I had a heart to reach people and wanted to find creative ways to share Christ with my friends. I wasn't very creative at the time and had no great ideas.

But I did one thing right. I would pray before school with a couple of friends. Then that group began to grow. Many of my friends became followers of Christ that year. The small youth group at my church grew like crazy—I will never forget how God moved that year.

When I finished high school, I was still looking for ways to reach people. As I prayed, God began to give me ideas and, looking to Him for strength, I began putting some of these ideas into action.

What I realized as I began serving my community is that I felt wonderful. Yes, it was challenging, frustrating, and exhausting at times, but I got a taste of ministry and as I saw lives changed, I was hooked. I wanted more.

I volunteered so much at my church that they put me on staff part-time. Eventually my calling became clear as I started full-time in a ministry career as an evangelist. However, I want to be really clear: I am called to ministry because I am a Christian. We all are. If you are a Christ-follower, you are called to ministry. We are all called to participate in the Great Commission (Matt. 28:18-20). It is not just reserved for pastors, evangelists, and professional Christians.

What is involved in the Great Commission (Matt. 28:18-20)?

In Matthew 28:18-20, "Jesus came near and said to them, 'All authority has been given to me in heaven and on earth. Go, therefore, and make disciples of all nations, baptizing them in the name of the Father and of the Son and of the Holy Spirit, teaching them to observe everything I have commanded you. And remember, I am with you always, to the end of the age.' "

Notice, Jesus said, "All authority has been given to me." Jesus, who had died just a few days before, stood there as the risen living God and gave the disciples a command: "Go."

What does it mean to "make disciples"?

To make disciples essentially means to replicate yourself, to multiply.

According to a study at Dallas Baptist University, by 325 A.D. it is estimated there were seven million Christians and two million martyrs—people who were killed because of their faith in Christ.[1]

How did the church go from a handful of people in Jerusalem to seven million people in just three centuries? Jesus said "go and make disciples" and that small group did just that. They made disciples, who made disciples, who then made disciples . . . see how this works? For the disciples, Jesus' words in Matthew 28:18-20 were not the Great Suggestion, but a serious mission. If you are a follower of Jesus, it's your mission to make disciples too.

Consider the story of the woman at the well. It was not culturally acceptable for a man to speak to a woman, especially if it was a Jewish man speaking to a Samaritan woman. The woman came to draw water from the well and Jesus began to speak to her. He quickly began to speak truth to her. She believed and immediately brought many of her friends to meet Jesus.

Jesus approached a total stranger because the opportunity presented itself. I believe if we ask God to give us opportunities to speak truth, He will place people in our paths so that we can share the good news with them.

GOD USES ORDINARY PEOPLE

You don't need special skills to do ministry. You simply need to be willing to be used by God. If you will humble yourself before Him, He will use you to bring others to Him. This is great news. God has called simply ordinary people like us to participate in His kingdom ministry.

I know what you are thinking. *But, I don't have the gift of evangelism so I don't share my faith.*

> ***Does that mean if you don't have the gift of giving, you shouldn't give? If you don't have the gift of prayer, you shouldn't pray?***

We have put too much emphasis on talented people doing successful ministry. God wants to use you right where you are!

> *And he himself gave some to be apostles, some prophets, some evangelists, some pastors and teachers, equipping the saints for the work of ministry, to build up the body of Christ —Ephesians 4:11-12*

We are all called to full-time ministry, whether we work a "Christian" job or not.

> ***If you could do anything to build the Kingdom, what would you do? What excites you? As you think about these things, what type of ministry do you see?***

What ministry opportunities interest and excite you? How might you begin engaging in this ministry right where you are?

You may have heard the saying, "Preach the gospel, use words when necessary." Well, let me make an announcement: Words are necessary. Yes, we should love people and live a life that represents Christ, but we need to open our mouths and speak the love of Christ and speak words of truth to point people to the cross. It is only there where they can find ultimate hope and the answer. Let's not be scared to open our mouths at the appropriate times and love people. It can be as simple as asking someone if you can pray for them when you know they are having a bad day.

I love art and creative projects. I also love adventure. I want to go to dangerous places, beautiful places, interesting places, hard to get places, and places that are gospel deprived. I love diverse cultures and weird food. All these things move me to go into unfamiliar places to share the gospel, places Egypt, or Greece, or Australia, or Central and South America.

I've had the opportunity to go to Alaska a few times. The last time, we went to the rural parts of western Alaska in remote villages that could only be accessed by ice roads. At one point I found myself driving on a frozen river, but we loved the adventure. It was great to finally get there and perform and speak in front of people who were so grateful to have visitors.

I also travel to Nicaragua often where I perform in prisons. These prisons have no running water, no electricity, no beds, no pillows, and no blankets. They are dark, filthy places. But I go and show love to the prisoners by performing and sharing the gospel with them.

When I see prisoners hear the gospel and respond with joy, I come alive. Ministry gives me life; it will make you come alive too.

Your goal should be to live out the Great Commission wherever God has planted you. He may one day send you to another country. But your focus right now should be on how you can build the Kingdom with what you have to offer.

He has given each person spiritual gifts to build His Kingdom. Each person is called to advance the gospel and go and make disciples.

You can't be a follower of Jesus and opt out of disciple making (Matt. 28:18-20). What Jesus wants from you is for you to be like Him. He was a disciple maker and wants us to be disciple makers. There is not a more direct command for us as followers. We are to go make disciples.

What are ways you can do ministry right now? At church? School? In your community?

How can you make a disciple?

A disciple pours his life into another person's life, who pours into another life.

There is a cycle of being a disciple and discipling someone.

If you are a Christ-follower, you are called to ministry. We are all called to participate in the Great Commission (Matt. 28:18-20).

Is it possible to be living in God's will and not a part of the Great Commission?

Would you rather have someone give you $10,000 per day for a month, or give you a penny the first day and then double your money every day thereafter (see chart below)?

- Day 1: $.01
- Day 2: $.02
- Day 3: $.04
- Day 4: $.08
- Day 5: $.16
- Day 6: $.32
- Day 7: $.64
- Day 8: $1.28
- Day 9: $2.56
- Day 10: $5.12

- Day 11: $10.24
- Day 12: $20.48
- Day 13: $40.96
- Day 14: $81.92
- Day 15: $163.84
- Day 16: $327.68
- Day 17: $655.36
- Day 18: $1,310.72
- Day 19: $2,621.44
- Day 20: $5,242.88

- Day 21: $10,485.76
- Day 22: $20,971.52
- Day 23: $41,943.04
- Day 24: $83,886.08
- Day 25: $167,772.16
- Day 26: $335,544.32
- Day 27: $671,088.64
- Day 28: $1,342,177.28
- Day 29: $2,684,354.56
- Day 30: $5,368,709.12

"The Great Commission is not merely to go to the ends of the earth preaching the gospel (Mark 16:15), nor to baptize a lot of converts into the name of the triune God, nor to teach them the precepts of Christ, but to 'make disciples'—to build people like themselves who were so constrained by the commission of Christ that they not only followed his way but led others to as well."[2]

AS HE PASSED ALONGSIDE THE SEA OF GALILEE, HE SAW SIMON AND
ANDREW, SIMON'S BROTHER, CASTING A NET INTO THE SEA—FOR THEY
WERE FISHERMEN. "FOLLOW ME," JESUS TOLD THEM, "AND I WILL MAKE
YOU FISH FOR PEOPLE." IMMEDIATELY THEY LEFT THEIR NETS AND
FOLLOWED HIM. GOING ON A LITTLE FARTHER, HE SAW JAMES THE SON
OF ZEBEDEE AND HIS BROTHER JOHN IN A BOAT PUTTING THEIR NETS IN
ORDER. IMMEDIATELY HE CALLED THEM, AND THEY LEFT THEIR FATHER
ZEBEDEE IN THE BOAT WITH THE HIRED MEN AND FOLLOWED HIM.

MARK 1:16-20

When I was 18 there was a commercial on TV for the Marines. The slogan was "a few good men." I later heard a friend of mine say that God was not looking for perfect people, or talented people, or the most intelligent people, but He just needs a few good men.

When God called the disciples, who did He choose? Average dudes. Nothing special. We know from Mark 1:16-20 that many of the disciples that Jesus called were fishermen. These were not highly educated or extremely qualified individuals. But they were called. They were obedient. They were available. Jesus was looking for a few good men and women. He was looking for people He could personally teach so they could replicate and multiply.

I remember when God called me to full-time ministry. I was already doing ministry with every opportunity at my university, and at work.

He began to get my attention. I realized He was looking for a "few good men."

That statement stuck with me. I realized that I am not perfect, but I am available to be used by God. Sign me up. You can sign up too! He wants to build His kingdom by using a few average men and women. That's you and I. Let's go. Let's obey His call.

Who does God want to use to build the kingdom?

Will you enlist? How you will you participate in and spread His kingdom?

JESUS CAME NEAR AND SAID TO THEM, "ALL AUTHORITY HAS BEEN GIVEN TO ME IN HEAVEN AND ON EARTH. GO, THEREFORE, AND MAKE DISCIPLES OF ALL NATIONS, BAPTIZING THEM IN THE NAME OF THE FATHER AND OF THE SON AND OF THE HOLY SPIRIT, TEACHING THEM TO OBSERVE EVERYTHING I HAVE COMMANDED YOU. AND REMEMBER, I AM WITH YOU ALWAYS, TO THE END OF THE AGE."

MATTHEW 28:18-20

What is ministry?

When Jesus was walking along the Sea of Galilee, He called some young men who were fishing and said, "Come follow me, and I will make you fish for men." They simply left their nets and followed Jesus and began loving and reaching people. They did everything they could to meet the physical needs of people. But most importantly, they pointed people to the truth. Jesus set a great example by both showing love and speaking truth.

Sometimes people get confused on this issue. Some people find it easy to feed the homeless or provide clothing for people in need. It's great to help people with physical things, but what do the people we serve need more than anything else? They need a relationship with God. Our acts of service should be coupled with speaking the truth of the gospel.

Ministry is always gospel-focused. If we give people food and water, but neglect to give them Christ—we've engaged in charity work, not missions. There is nothing wrong with helping people, but true ministry involves spreading the good news of salvation that is only found in Jesus Christ. What good is it to help someone with a physical need and ignore their spiritual need? We must do both.

READ MATTHEW 28:18-20 AGAIN.

Jesus and His disciples were devoted to ministry—they loved people and spoke truth to them. When Jesus left the disciples, He left them with the command to go, make disciples, baptize them, and teach them all He had commanded. Ministry can be summed up in this statement: Show love, speak truth.

What is one way you could engage in ministry in your school or neighborhood?

Who will you show love and speak truth to this week?

ACCORDING TO THE GRACE GIVEN TO US, WE HAVE DIFFERENT GIFTS: IF PROPHECY, USE IT ACCORDING TO THE PROPORTION OF ONE'S FAITH; IF SERVICE, USE IT IN SERVICE; IF TEACHING, IN TEACHING; IF EXHORTING, IN EXHORTATION; GIVING, WITH GENEROSITY; LEADING, WITH DILIGENCE; SHOWING MERCY, WITH CHEERFULNESS.

ROMANS 12:6-8

God gave you gifts. It's like Christmas morning. You need to open the paper wrapping and discover what He has given you.

God uses people to carry out ministry. How does He do this? He has given every follower spiritual gifts. You are to use those gifts to minister to other people. Those in your church and in the community should be receiving ministry from you as you use your gifts. And you should also be empowered by others using their gifts to minister to you.

All Christ followers possess gifts for ministry. They are called spiritual gifts. They are what God has given us in order for us to build the Kingdom. Here are some examples:

- 1 Corinthians 12:8-10
- 1 Corinthians 12:28
- Ephesians 4:11

You can find your spiritual gift by serving in different ways as needs and opportunities arise. As you serve, you will notice that some things come naturally. Some things will give you great joy. Pay attention to what these things are and let your gifts grow and develop.

What are your spiritual gifts? Name 2-3 things that rise to the top.

What is one practical way you could use one of your spiritual gifts to help or serve someone this week?

Pray for strength to begin using your gifts deliberately and consistently to serve others and build Christ's kingdom.

BUT YOU WILL RECEIVE POWER WHEN THE HOLY SPIRIT HAS COME
ON YOU, AND YOU WILL BE MY WITNESSES IN JERUSALEM, IN ALL
JUDEA AND SAMARIA, AND TO THE END OF THE EARTH.

ACTS 1:8

When should I start?

You may be asking yourself, "When can I start?" Maybe you should wait to start until you are older? Maybe you should wait until you know the Bible inside and out?

You don't need to reach top-level spiritual status before you can be used by God. Start serving right where you are and allow God to work through you in your home, school, and community. I see many Christians who say, "I'll wait until I am a mature Christian," or "I'll wait until I get properly trained," or "I'll wait until I have my life all figured out." Some never start for fear of failure. Some never start for fear of being embarrassed. We need to get past our fears. Such fears are tools used by the enemy to paralyze you and make you ineffective. If you have been saved by God, then you are ready. You can serve, love, and share your testimony of God's work in your life.

God wants to use ordinary people like you and me to build the kingdom. He even promised to give us power in the Spirit to enable us to be effective. Look at what He tells the disciples right before He left them to start their mission. Read Acts 1:8 again.

We are His witnesses. He will give us power through the Holy Spirit. Know this and act on it.

When the apostle Paul was saved by Jesus, he immediately began to tell people about the change in his life. He didn't do everything right; he was far from perfect. But God used him. Ananias helped disciple him in those early years, but Paul was eager to point people to Christ.

What are you waiting for? What is holding you back from engaging in ministry?

If you keep coming up with things you ought to do before you start doing ministry, you'll never get started. Start now and then develop your gifts as you go.

What's holding you back from sharing your testimony with a friend? What's holding you back from serving or volunteering in your church? Or community?

WHATEVER YOU DO, DO IT FROM THE HEART, AS SOMETHING DONE FOR THE LORD AND NOT FOR PEOPLE, KNOWING THAT YOU WILL RECEIVE THE REWARD OF AN INHERITANCE FROM THE LORD. YOU SERVE THE LORD CHRIST.

COLOSSIANS 3:23-24

Where should I start? The good news is that you can start where you are right now.

Some people can get bogged down with the idea of having to go to a place to do ministry. Maybe it's going to Africa to work with orphans, or on a mission trip to a needy or unreached people group far away. These are all good things but you don't need to start there. Start at home, at school, at work and, most importantly, at your church.

If you are not currently doing ministry in some way, you need to re-examine the New Testament. Ministry is essential to following Jesus. Start where you are. A college professor of mine used to say, "Bloom where you are planted." Jesus told the disciples in Acts 1:8 that they would start in Jerusalem and then branch out to the ends of the earth. Start locally before you think globally.

> *Read Colossians 3:23-24 again and think about the things you do on a day-to-day basis and how you can do the smallest of things for the glory of God.*

I was saved when I was in tenth grade. I did not have a seminary degree or a certificate on the wall. I was just a knucklehead teenager who had a heart to serve Jesus. I started doing ministry in my hometown right away. I began praying with friends and reading Scripture with them. I would invite others who were not followers of Christ to join us. I would find creative ways to introduce Jesus to other people. Later I got a little more bold and started to talk to strangers about Jesus. I didn't do a great job, I didn't get it totally right all of the time, but God used me and my friends. Later in life I began to search for other ways to serve in ministry. I now have a ministry that takes me to many different countries around the world but it all started in high school. I've made lots of mistakes along the way but God has used my mistakes to help me grow. I will never regret doing ministry in my small rural town in Louisiana.

> *Where should you start? Draw a circle around your house, school, or church. Start there.*

> *List a few ways you will start sharing Jesus there this week.*

SO WE DO NOT FOCUS ON WHAT IS SEEN, BUT ON WHAT IS UNSEEN. FOR
WHAT IS SEEN IS TEMPORARY, BUT WHAT IS UNSEEN IS ETERNAL.

2 CORINTHIANS 4:18

How should I get started?

Look for opportunities. If you ask God to give you an opportunity to show love and/or speak truth, He will do it. He wants to use you and He will show you ways you can be used right where you are. He will not ask you to preach a sermon if you aren't ready. God equips and empowers us as we grow. He promises to work through us as we use the spiritual gifts He has given us. I recommend starting small and doing something in your circle of influence.

It starts with opening our eyes. If we walk around blindly and not noticing the world around us, we will miss opportunities to love, serve, and point others to Christ. Be aware of the hurting world around you. Ask God to help you take notice of someone who is broken or in need. When someone is upset or isolates themselves, simply talk to them. Take initiative.

Maybe you will notice a problem or a spiritual need in the community. Maybe it is something that keeps coming up. When you find yourself thinking about that person or need over and over again, then it might just be the Holy Spirit showing you that it's time to act.

Be careful though, for not all problems in the world are ours to solve.

There was a missionary in Central America who posted a picture of a poor neighborhood that she was working in. Some people in the U.S. noticed the dogs in the picture. The dogs were skinny and uncared for. Some people wanted to send money to help save the dogs. They totally missed out on the fact that it was the children who were starving. Remember who and what is most important. If you are searching and praying for God to use you, then I can promise you He will do it. Remember to show love and speak truth, and let's build the kingdom of God together.

> *How can we serve our church today? How can we show love to a friend in need?*
> *How can we love our community?*

> *How will you prioritize your time and energy to serve God and point people*
> *to Christ?*

SESSION 8

COMMUNITY

# VIDEO ——
GUIDE

Start by watching the video for Session 8. Not only did the cards in the illusion change, but the girls and guys involved in the illusion also changed. Brock gives us a behind-the-scenes look and describes how it took an entire crew, a community to make it happen.

IN THE SAME WAY, SPIRITUAL GROWTH REQUIRES COMMUNITY—IT TAKES THE ENTIRE BODY OF BELIEVERS, NOT JUST US.

> *How would you describe biblical community?*

> *Is this something you strive to make a part of your life and walk with Christ? Why or why not?*

Brock shares about a time as a teen when he was depressed and isolated in order to explain the importance of community. He went to a youth camp and it was there he saw true biblical community and surrendered his life to Christ. He encourages us to not just go to church, but to be the church. Don't be an island, but be a community. Just as Jesus had a community of disciples, we need to surround ourselves with a community of believers.

> *Do you have a church and a community of believers who you can share and talk about God with?*

> *Why is this so important? How has biblical community benefited you personally?*

> *How can you encourage others in your community this week?*

As you wrap up the final session of this study, ask God to give you a deep desire for Him and the strength necessary to faithfully practice the spiritual disciplines. Take time to pray, read God's Word, serve, and spend some time in solitude this week. If you are not already a part of a community of believers, seek to find a group of believers in your church this week.

THERE WAS A TIME WHEN MY WIFE AND I MOVED OUT OF OUR TOWNHOUSE AND INTO A BUS TO TRAVEL THE WORLD. We left everything behind and packed what we could into our diesel recreational vehicle (RV) and toured full-time from city to city. We saw the Grand Canyon and Mount Rushmore, Niagara Falls, and the white beaches of Florida. We even saw the rainforest in Washington state. After each show, we would look at the map and determine the most scenic route to the next show as we toured. It was wonderful. But, something was missing. We wondered why it began to feel lonely even though we were together and experiencing such great memories. One day a friend of mine said to me something that got my attention. He said, "you need community." I was shaken by that simple statement. Intuitively I knew that I needed community, but I had no idea what that looked like.

What is community? How would you define it?

Rick Howerton in his book, *A Different Kind of Tribe* (2012), says that community is a shared common life. Rick defines it as having a shared language, experiences, goals, and expectations.

Biblical community is a lifestyle that is different than that of the world. We are becoming like Christ, and living out the model He showed us.

Scripture calls us, as believers, to share life together. We were created for community. Even before the world existed, community did. The triune God—Father, Son, and Holy Spirit—existed and created the universe. When God created Adam, He immediately said that it's not good for him to be alone; therefore, He made Eve as his companion.

How does the Bible define community?

Later in Scripture, God established the importance of community for His people. He gave Aaron to Moses to walk alongside him as he led the people out of Egypt and into the promised land. Jesus lived in community. He walked with 12 men, the apostles, and an even closer, more intimate community with three of them. In Acts 2:42-47, the disciples lived together in community when the church began to explode. In each of his missionary journeys, Paul was never alone—he always brought others with him to share the work. In Acts 13, for example, God provided companions to walk with Paul in particularly tough places of ministry. There is accountability and power in the community God designs for us. Even when Jesus returns, He is not merely coming back for you individually, He is coming for the church, His global community of faith.

Most of Paul's letters were written to communities. Granted, they were broken communities; but, nonetheless communities of people who had trusted Jesus to save them. We were not meant to follow Christ by ourselves. We are not islands. We are individual parts of the greater body of

Christ called to live and work together (see 1 Cor. 12:14). Look at 1 Corinthians 12:26 and you will see that we are carrying the load together. If one suffers, all suffer; if one member is honored, all rejoice together!

Following Christ means committing to His body, the church. This means we are in this together, through the good, the bad, and the ugly. And believe me, it will get ugly.

When a brother or sister is down, we are there to help lift them up. When we fall or face tragedy, we have others to help lift us up through love, support, prayer, accountability, and encouragement.

When a new believer comes into the faith family, God provides a community in which the infant can grow. We all need examples—we need to show each other what it looks like to follow Jesus.

Why is community so important?

Community gives us accountability, power, unity, faithfulness to Scripture, and security.

Life-transforming community is often found in small groups. In small groups, you can get to know people; you can look people in the eye. In big groups, you must sit in rows. If you are sitting in a row, the best you can do is look at the back of someone's head or turn or look at the person beside you. Sitting in a circle allows you to see people's faces.

How can we develop deep, honest, life-giving relationships with other believers?

The more time we spend face-to-face, the better we will know each other and the more willing we will be to open up to one another.

My point is this: when we sit in a small group circle with the same people a few times a month, or more, then we will get to know them and they will know us. There will be an obvious lifestyle that will develop.

BIBLICAL COMMUNITY

True biblical community is tied to a biblical lifestyle. A group of believers in a small group with biblical community will be growing together to become more like Jesus. That's church!

Much of what I have learned over the years has come from my close Christian friends. Living life together gives me a chance to see God working in their lives, as well as God showing them things in my life that will help all of us grow. This is not to put down biblical teaching from a teacher or pastor on Sunday morning. In fact, this is the extension of that teaching.

In my own church community, we meet at someone's house once a week and discuss and apply our pastor's sermon from the previous Sunday. We share our struggles, share wisdom and encouragement, and we pray for each other. It's a powerful time that I look forward to each week.

If you take a deep look at Acts 2:42-47, you will find a few interesting characteristics of community. Here are just a few that stood out to me.

- They devoted themselves to the teaching.
- They broke bread. Dinner time!
- They prayed together.
- They were giving money and possessions to those in need.
- They were praising God together.

The following are four characteristics of community:

- Common Language
- Common Memories
- Common Traditions
- Common Vision of Community

Jim Rohn famously said, "You are the average of the five people you spend the most time with."[1]

We spend time with our family at home and friends at school or work, and they are constantly rubbing off on us. In the same way, you are rubbing off on them in a small way. We must choose carefully who we do life with.

You need to be intentional about cultivating close community with those who are growing in the faith. The more solid our faith community is, the more solid we will be.

If your closest friends spend time talking about Jesus, acting like Jesus, quoting Jesus, singing songs about Jesus, and so on, then I imagine you would begin to follow that pattern. Eventually, you would become a little more like your friends and a little more like Jesus.

We live in a world that has less and less biblical influence on our culture and fewer people talking about or acting anything like Jesus. We need help from the Lord but also from each other!

When has God used biblical community to encourage you or to point you back to Him and His Word? Explain.

How can you grow in community with other believers?

Who in your life needs help, encouragement, or accountability in their walk with Christ? How might you help them?

There have been times in my life when I was at my weakest and most vulnerable state and I was not sure what would happen next. It was during those times that my faith community lifted me up and gave me a way to get back on my feet. This only happens in community.

THE IMPORTANCE OF COMMUNITY

When you graduate high school and go to college or start a career, it is a vulnerable time. If you watch a person choose their community, you can usually see where their life will be in a few years. If you choose to live in a house with people who spend all their time drinking and partying, there is a good chance you will eventually become just like them. On the other hand, if you connect yourself with a group of people who are in the Word, praying, and doing ministry, then you will be far more likely to do the same.

It's not possible to overstate the value and impact of Christlike community. Search for it. Don't give up until you find it. You were never meant to follow Jesus on your own.

We were not meant to follow Christ by ourselves. We are not islands. We are individual parts of the greater body of Christ called to live and work together.

LEADER GUIDE

THANK YOU for your commitment to teach spiritual disciplines to students. Each of these seven disciplines we cover in this study are absolutely essential to spiritual growth. It is our hope and prayer that God will use this study to draw students into a deep and abiding relationship with His Son so that they might make a massive impact for His kingdom in their homes, schools, neighborhoods, and to the ends of the earth.

The Leader Guide is designed to help you prepare for each session and equip you with additional tools, questions, and activities as you lead students to unpack the value of each of the seven disciplines.

HOW DOES THE LEADER GUIDE WORK?

The Leader Guide is broken up into four short sections: (1) Main Point, (2) Getting Started, (3) Press Play, and (4) On Your Own.

MAIN POINT

We've included the Main Point of each session at the beginning of each Leader Guide to help you stay focused and on task. You will want to repeat this phrase early and often to your students as you guide them through each session.

GETTING STARTED

This section will give you some tips for opening the session through ice breakers, illustrations, or simple activities that introduce the main point of each session.

PRESS PLAY

After Getting Started, you will simply Press Play and watch each session's video with your students. Make sure your video system is set up and working prior to each session.

ON YOUR OWN

This section provides a personal challenge for students to either engage in the spiritual discipline highlighted in the session or how to prepare to do so. There are a couple different ways you can approach this section. You may want to encourage students to take their books home and complete this section on their own. Groups with more time, however, may decide to have students complete this section at the end of each group meeting.

I SAY THEN, WALK BY THE SPIRIT AND YOU WILL CERTAINLY NOT CARRY OUT THE DESIRE OF THE FLESH. FOR THE FLESH DESIRES WHAT IS AGAINST THE SPIRIT, AND THE SPIRIT DESIRES WHAT IS AGAINST THE FLESH; THESE ARE OPPOSED TO EACH OTHER, SO THAT YOU DON'T DO WHAT YOU WANT. BUT IF YOU ARE LED BY THE SPIRIT, YOU ARE NOT UNDER THE LAW.

GALATIANS 5:16-18

Main Point: Every believer has two natures—the spirit and the flesh. Feed the spirit and starve the flesh.

Getting Started: Start your study by breaking students up into pairs. Give each pair a sheet of paper and a pen or pencil. Guide them to pretend they are about to start training to run a marathon (26.2 miles). Instruct them to jot down a plan for how they would prepare to run a marathon, listing things like what they would eat, how they would train, and how often and how far they would run. After students have had a few minutes to compile their plan, ask a few pairs to share their plan with the rest of the group. Point out that significant tasks like running a marathon require careful planning and preparation. The same is true for our spiritual lives. If we hope to grow in Christ, we must commit ourselves to training in godliness. Today we will discover that everything we do is training of some sort—training that either feeds our flesh or the Spirit who dwells within all believers. It's time to feed the dog—it's time to feed the spirit as we seek to make the spiritual disciplines a regular part of our everyday lives.

Press Play: Set up and make sure the video system is working in advance so that it is ready for you to simply press play. Watch the Session 1 video (included in the DVD Kit). Allow time for discussion after using the discussion questions on page 7.

On Your Own: Give each student a sheet of paper or a notecard and a pen or pencil. On their sheet, instruct them to jot down an answer to the following three questions. After students have finished answering the questions, take up their papers and keep them somewhere safe so that you can return it to them during the last week of this study. Promise them that you will not read their answers.

- What regular practices are essential to growing in Christ?
- Which of these practices are you most comfortable with? Most uncomfortable with?
- What are the biggest barriers in your life standing between you and growing in your relationship with Christ?

Notes:

THEREFORE,
BROTHERS AND
SISTERS, IN VIEW
OF THE MERCIES OF
GOD, I URGE YOU
TO PRESENT YOUR
BODIES AS A LIVING
SACRIFICE, HOLY AND
PLEASING TO GOD;
THIS IS YOUR TRUE
WORSHIP. DO NOT
BE CONFORMED TO
THIS AGE, BUT BE
TRANSFORMED BY THE
RENEWING OF YOUR
MIND, SO THAT YOU
MAY DISCERN WHAT IS
THE GOOD, PLEASING,
AND PERFECT
WILL OF GOD.

*ROMANS
12:1-2*

Main Point: Worship is the response we give God based on our love for Him because of who He is and what He has already done. Worship feeds the dog; worship feeds the Spirit.

Getting Started: Go around the room and ask each student to share their favorite actor, musician, or athlete. Once each student has shared, ask several students to share more about their favorite person. What is she or he like? What are his or her interests, passions, goals, beliefs, or desires? As students struggle to answer some of these rather personal questions, point out that to truly love or appreciate someone, you need to know more than just a few facts about them. The same is true of our relationship with God. In order to truly worship Him as He deserves, we need to know more than merely just a few facts about Him. We need to know His character, His heart, His goals and passions. This week we will be challenged to engage in the discipline of worship which provides the foundation for all the other disciplines. In fact, the very point of engaging in spiritual disciplines is to love and treasure God more—to worship. When we dig deeper than merely uncovering a few facts about God and commit to know His heart, we will find ourselves worshiping Him more and more. And we will find the Spirit of Christ in us growing such that we begin living and becoming more and more like our Savior.

Press Play: Set up and make sure the video system is working in advance so that it is ready for you to simply press play. Watch the Session 2 video (included in the DVD Kit). Allow time for discussion after using the discussion questions on page 19.

On Your Own: Give each student a notecard and a pen or pencil. On their sheet, instruct them to compile a list of God's attributes: holy, loving, gracious, just, and so on. Once they have compiled their list, encourage them to keep this notecard in their pocket or in their purse throughout the week. Instruct them to say a short prayer praising God based on one of His attributes every time they refer to the card this week.

Notes:

HOW CAN A YOUNG
MAN KEEP HIS WAY
PURE? BY KEEPING
YOUR WORD. I HAVE
SOUGHT YOU WITH
ALL MY HEART;
DON'T LET ME
WANDER FROM YOUR
COMMANDS. I HAVE
TREASURED YOUR
WORD IN MY HEART
SO THAT I MAY NOT
SIN AGAINST YOU.

*PSALM
119:9-11*

Main Point: If you want to hear God's voice and know His will, you need to study His Word. Scripture feeds the dog; Scripture feeds the Spirit.

Getting Started: Play "Two Truths and a Lie" with your group. Select a few students to share three things about themselves, these could include places they have visited, experiences they have had, accomplishments, or things they have done. Tell the students who are participating to make one of the things a lie—something that they haven't actually done or isn't actually true of them. The other students in your group will then try to determine which of the three things is a lie. You will likely have a few students who guess correctly but more often than not they will be wrong. Point out that to truly know another person, you have to spend time with them, ask questions, and listen. However, even then, there is still much we don't know about each other. Point out that there is much your students do not yet know about God. However, thankfully He has not left us in the dark about who He is and what He is about. God's Word, the Bible, informs us of His heart, His character, and His will for our lives. Hearing God's voice and living out His will starts with humbly studying His Word, the Bible.

Press Play: Set up and make sure the video system is working in advance so that it is ready for you to simply press play. Watch the Session 3 video (included in the DVD Kit). Allow time for discussion after using the discussion questions on page 31.

On Your Own: Read Psalm 119:1-16 and compile a list as you go:

* Make a list of how God's Word is described in these verses.
* Make a list of the benefits that come from studying and applying God's Word to your life.
* Designate a time each day this week when you will complete the daily devotions in this book and spend some time reading the Bible.

Notes:

THIS IS THE
CONFIDENCE WE
HAVE BEFORE HIM:
IF WE ASK ANYTHING
ACCORDING TO HIS
WILL, HE HEARS US.

*1 JOHN
5:14*

BUT WHEN YOU
PRAY, GO INTO YOUR
PRIVATE ROOM, SHUT
YOUR DOOR, AND
PRAY TO YOUR FATHER
WHO IS IN SECRET.
AND YOUR FATHER
WHO SEES IN SECRET
WILL REWARD YOU.

*MATTHEW
6:6*

Main Point: Prayer is not a magic charm, a performance, or a secret formula. Prayer is when a child of God talks to his or her heavenly Father. Prayer feeds the dog; prayer feeds the Spirit.

Getting Started: Ask students to close their eyes and imagine that someone they admire, perhaps their favorite musician, athlete, or actor. Once each student has someone in mind, with eyes closed, tell them to pretend this person just walked unexpectedly into the room. What would you say? How would you feel? Would you be nervous? Do you think you might second guess your words? Tell students to open their eyes. Point out how we get nervous in the presence of famous, powerful, or admirable people. If someone you greatly looked up to came into the room, you might just be at a loss for words. The same is sometimes true in our relationship with God; we hesitate to pray to Him because we are afraid we will fumble our words or fail to impress Him with our words. Read Luke 18:9-14 and help students see that the goal of prayer is not to impress God but to connect with Him and be honest with Him. What honors God is not fancy words but a humble heart. Prayer is not a performance but an opportunity to talk with our heavenly Father who loves us and sent His Son to die for us.

Press Play: Set up and make sure the video system is working in advance so that it is ready for you to simply press play. Watch the Session 4 video (included in the DVD Kit). Allow time for discussion after using the discussion questions on page 43.

On Your Own: Guide students to pray with a partner before they leave your group meeting. Try not to give too much direction as to what they should pray about. If they struggle to think of things to pray for, remind them that prayer is simply conversation with the God who loves us and died for us. In other words, just be honest with God, ask for His help, and pray that He would help you love Him and live for Him. If you do not have time for students to pray together, send each student in your group a text message this week asking them how you can pray for them and sharing a prayer request of your own.

Notes:

VERY EARLY IN THE MORNING, WHILE IT WAS STILL DARK, HE GOT UP, WENT OUT, AND MADE HIS WAY TO A DESERTED PLACE; AND THERE HE WAS PRAYING.

MARK 1:35

YET HE OFTEN WITHDREW TO DESERTED PLACES AND PRAYED.

LUKE 5:16

DURING THOSE DAYS HE WENT OUT TO THE MOUNTAIN TO PRAY AND SPENT ALL NIGHT IN PRAYER TO GOD.

LUKE 6:12

Main Point: Solitude is purposefully spending time alone in silence. It's not being lonely, it's being alone with the intention of meeting with God. Solitude feeds the dog; solitude feeds the Spirit.

Getting Started: Instruct students to sit in a circle. Ask every student who has a phone to take it out of their bag or pocket. If their phone is on silent or vibrate, tell them to turn the ringer on and the volume all the way up. All students can play, whether they have a phone or not. The goal of the game is not to look at their phone or anyone else's for one minute. Encourage students to look each other in the eye without glancing down. Tell students to keep an eye on each other and to speak up if they see someone glance down at any one of the phones. You might even have another adult, during the game, send out text messages or other notifications to the group to make the game even more difficult. After a minute is up, whoever has not looked at one of the phones is a winner. Repeat the game as you have time. Afterward, point out that we live in an age of constant distraction. In this game, you were constantly tempted to look down at the phones because text messaging and social media have trained us to constantly look at our phones. Jesus didn't have a cell phone but that doesn't mean He wasn't surrounded by constant distraction. People were constantly begging for His attention and yet Jesus prioritized times of solitude during His earthly ministry. We too need to unplug from distractions and get alone with God. We need solitude. It's one of the practices God has given us to feed the dog—solitude helps us grow in Christ.

Press Play: Set up and make sure the video system is working in advance so that it is ready for you to simply press play. Watch the Session 5 video (included in the DVD Kit). Allow time for discussion after using the discussion questions on page 55.

On Your Own: Close your group time with a moment of silence. Challenge students to simply sit quietly for one minute, thinking about what they have learned about God and about spiritual growth in this session. Challenge students to practice the discipline of solitude this week by simply finding a place in their home where they can be alone for a few minutes each day this week. Encourage them to report back to you about their experience next week.

Notes:

"WHENEVER YOU FAST, DON'T BE GLOOMY LIKE THE HYPOCRITES. FOR THEY MAKE THEIR FACES UNATTRACTIVE SO THAT THEIR FASTING IS OBVIOUS TO PEOPLE. TRULY I TELL YOU, THEY HAVE THEIR REWARD. BUT WHEN YOU FAST, PUT OIL ON YOUR HEAD AND WASH YOUR FACE, SO THAT YOUR FASTING ISN'T OBVIOUS TO OTHERS BUT TO YOUR FATHER WHO IS IN SECRET. AND YOUR FATHER WHO SEES IN SECRET WILL REWARD YOU..

MATTHEW 6:16-18

Main Point: The purpose of fasting is to grow in our dependence on God. We are all in desperate need of God—fasting helps us realize this and live in light of this truth. Fasting feeds the dog; fasting feeds the Spirit.

Getting Started: Share with your students about the hungriest you have ever been. Make sure your example is not one of fasting so that you don't fall into the trap that Jesus warned about in Matthew 6:16-18. Ask a few students to share their own example of serious hunger. What might we learn from such times? What does the fact that we all need and long for food on a regular basis tell us about ourselves? Point out that our need for food demonstrates something really important about our nature as human beings, namely that we are needy. Unlike God who is self-sufficient, we are needy creatures. We can't go more than a few hours without thinking about our desire for food. We all have a deeper need, however, than our need for food—our need for God. Our greatest need, even greater than our need for food, water, or shelter, is to connect with the God who made us. Fasting therefore, is not a practice of punishing ourselves in some weird attempt to make ourselves more holy. Fasting is a reminder that we are needy and weak. It reminds us of who we truly are and how dependent we are on God for everything. When we fast humbly, it challenges us to connect more deeply and fervently with God in prayer and Bible study. Fasting does not feed your physical body but it does feed your Spirit; it helps you seek God.

Press Play: Set up and make sure the video system is working in advance so that it is ready for you to simply press play. Watch the Session 6 video (included in the DVD Kit). Allow time for discussion after using the discussion questions on page 67.

On Your Own: Most of your students probably have not fasted before. Challenge them to fast for a short period of time this week. It doesn't have to be a full day, it could just be one meal. It's okay to start small. Encourage them to seek God in prayer and Bible study during the time they would have been eating. Be very careful, however, as some of them may have struggled with eating disorders in the past. Therefore instruct students very clearly to talk about their fasting with a parent or trusted adult in the faith to make sure it's appropriate for them.

Notes:

JESUS CAME NEAR
AND SAID TO THEM,
"ALL AUTHORITY
HAS BEEN GIVEN
TO ME IN HEAVEN
AND ON EARTH. GO,
THEREFORE, AND
MAKE DISCIPLES
OF ALL NATIONS,
BAPTIZING THEM IN
THE NAME OF THE
FATHER AND OF
THE SON AND OF
THE HOLY SPIRIT,
TEACHING THEM TO
OBSERVE EVERYTHING
I HAVE COMMANDED
YOU. AND REMEMBER,
I AM WITH YOU
ALWAYS, TO THE
END OF THE AGE."

MATTHEW 28:18-20

Main Point: You don't need special skills or experience to be used by God. All followers of Jesus are called to ministry—to use the gifts God has given them to serve the church and build Christ's kingdom. Ministry feeds the dog; ministry feeds the Spirit.

Getting Started: Instruct students to sit in a circle as you begin your group discussion time. Go around the circle and ask each student to share one nice thing about the student sitting directly across the circle from them. Even if they don't know each other, they can at least say something nice about that person. Next ask for a few volunteers to share a verse of the Bible that has impacted him or her in the past and helped him or her to follow Christ. After students are finished sharing, point out that saying something nice, in a small way, is actually a form of ministry. Sometimes we make ministry out to be "bigger" things like preaching, teaching, and missions. One of the spiritual gifts Paul mentions in Romans 12:7-8 is the gift of encouragement. A timely word of kindness or sharing God's Word with someone are simple examples of practicing this gift. These acts are ministry. Today you will help students see that they don't have to have a Bible degree or jump through a set of spiritual hoops to be used by God to build His church and advance His kingdom. We are all called to ministry.

Press Play: Set up and make sure the video system is working in advance so that it is ready for you to simply press play. Watch the Session 7 video (included in the DVD Kit). Allow time for discussion after using the discussion questions on page 79.

On Your Own: Give students a challenge as they go home to talk to their parents or a trusted Christian mentor this week (perhaps this is you) about their spiritual gifts. Encourage them to ask this person what spiritual gifts they see in you and how they might exercise this gift for the good of the church.

Notes:

THEY DEVOTED
THEMSELVES TO
THE APOSTLES'
TEACHING, TO THE
FELLOWSHIP, TO THE
BREAKING OF BREAD,
AND TO PRAYER...

NOW ALL THE
BELIEVERS WERE
TOGETHER AND
HELD ALL THINGS IN
COMMON. THEY SOLD
THEIR POSSESSIONS
AND PROPERTY AND
DISTRIBUTED THE
PROCEEDS TO ALL, AS
ANY HAD NEED. EVERY
DAY THEY DEVOTED
THEMSELVES TO
MEETING TOGETHER
IN THE TEMPLE, AND
BROKE BREAD FROM
HOUSE TO HOUSE.

*ACTS 2:42,
44-46*

Main Point: We were created for community. Following Christ means committing to His body, the church. Community feeds the dog; community feeds the Spirit.

Getting Started: Bring identical sets of children's jigsaw puzzles to your group meeting. Have a group of 4-5 students race to finish one puzzle while another student races against them to finish the other puzzle alone. Make sure no one helps the student who is working alone. When the group finishes first, point out how the game was unfair from the beginning. This silly game, however, confirms an important spiritual truth—we are better together. God created us for community. If you or your students try to live the Christian life on your own, you will fail. We need each other. God calls us to live in community, cheering each other on in our faith and helping one another pursue Christ.

Press Play: Set up and make sure the video system is working in advance so that it is ready for you to simply press play. Watch the Session 7 video (included in the DVD Kit). Allow time for discussion after using the discussion questions on page 91.

On Your Own: The challenge this week is a little unique as this is our last session in *Feed the Dog*. Challenge students to find a time to get together with another student from your group this week for the purpose of praying together. It could be at lunch at school or perhaps a few minutes before church. Remind them that living in community is more than just hanging out, it involves intentionally helping each other pursue Jesus.

Return their papers from Session 1 and give them time to reflect on their answers and discuss how they might answer these questions differently now that they've finished this study.

Notes:

SOURCES

SESSION 1
1. Frederick F. Bruce, *Paul: Apostle of the Heart Set Free* (Grand Rapids: Wm. B. Eerddmans Publishing Co., 2000), 206.
2. Joan B. Smith, *Got Contentment?* (Xulon Press, 2008), 32.

SESSION 2
1. Oswald Chambers, "Worship," My Utmost For His Highest, accessed July 25, 2017. https://utmost.org/worship/
2. "Worship," Webster's 1913 Dictionary, accessed July 25, 2017. http://www.webster-dictionary.org/definition/worship

SESSION 3
1. John Foxe, *Foxe's book of martyrs: a complete and authentic account of the lives, suffering, and triumphant deaths of the primitive and Protestant martyrs in all parts of the world* (London: Knight and Son, 1856), 152.
2. Joan Minninger, *Total Recall: How to Maximize Your Memory Power* (MJF Books, 1993), 3.
3. Warren W. Wiersbe, *The Wiersbe Bible Commentary: New Testament*, (David C. Cook: Colorado Springs, 2007), 296.
4. Robert Noland, "Our Mess vs. His Mind," The Knight's Code (blog), accessed July 25, 2017, http://theknightscode.com/2017/04/mess-vs-mind/

SESSION 5
1. Jason Thibeault, "Quotes," Jason Thibeault (blog), accessed July 25, 2017, http://jasonthibeault.com/quotes/albert-einstein/
2. "Tesla > Quotes > Quotable Quote," *Goodreads* [online], accessed July 25, 2017. Available from the internet: https://www.goodreads.com/quotes/12601-the-mind-is-sharper-and-keener-in-seclusion-and-uninterrupted.
3. "Pablo Picasso > Quotes > Quotable Quote," *Goodreads* [online], accessed July 25, 2017. Available from the internet: https://www.goodreads.com/quotes/629534-without-great-solitude-no-serious-work-is-possible.

SESSION 6
1. Mark Mattson, "Why fasting bolsters brain power: Mark Mattson at TEDxJohnsHopkinsUniversity." Posted March 18,2014 by TEDx Talks. https://www.youtube.com/watch?v=4UkZAwKoCP8
2. ibid.
3. David Mathis, *Habits of Grace: Enjoying Jesus through the Spiritual Disciplines* (Crossway: Wheaton, 2016), https://books.google.com/books?id=ySGNCwAAQBAJ&pg=PT96&dq=habits+of+grace+enjoying+jesus+this+much,+o+god&hl=en&sa=X&ved=0ahUKEwjr7pOHwrfVAhVGOyYKHckNCs0Q6AEIKzAB#v=onepage&q=habits%20of%20grace%20enjoying%20jesus%20this%20much%2C%20o%20god&f=false

SESSION 7
1. Ancient Christian Martyrdom: A Brief Overview, Dallas Baptist University, accessed July 25, 2017. http://www3.dbu.edu/mitchell/anceint_christian_martyrdom.htm
2. Robert E. Coleman, *The Master Plan of Evangelism, Second Edition, Abridged* (Grand Rapids: Baker Publishing Group, 2010), 104.

SESSION 8
1. "Jim Rohn > Quotes > Quotable Quote," *Goodreads* [online], accessed July 25, 2017. Available from the internet: https://www.goodreads.com/quotes/1798-you-are-the-average-of-the-five-people-you-spend.